SUPER SAD UNICORN: A MEMOIR OF MANIA

SUPER SAD UNICORN

A MEMOIR OF MANIA

JESSICA EKHOFF

NEW DEGREE PRESS

COPYRIGHT © 2023 JESSICA EKHOFF

All rights reserved.

SUPER SAD UNICORN

A Memoir of Mania

ISBN   979-8-88926-610-5   *Paperback*
            979-8-88926-611-2   *Ebook*

For Dane, the best person I'll ever know.

And for everyone at AMITA Health Alexian Brothers Perinatal Intensive Outpatient Therapy Program, for helping me find myself again.

CONTENTS

	AUTHOR'S NOTE	9
CHAPTER 1.	WAITING FOR WELLS	11
CHAPTER 2.	CAREER COACH	21
CHAPTER 3.	JAUNDICE	29
CHAPTER 4.	RAGE	33
CHAPTER 5.	BRINGING IN THE REINFORCEMENTS	43
CHAPTER 6.	UNRAVELING	55
CHAPTER 7.	DIVERSITY	65
CHAPTER 8.	PROVING MYSELF	77
CHAPTER 9.	THE INTERVIEW	85
CHAPTER 10.	FIGHTING FOR THE LITTLE GUY	99
CHAPTER 11.	THE BREAKDOWN	105
CHAPTER 12.	INTAKE	115
CHAPTER 13.	SUPER SAD UNICORN	125
CHAPTER 14.	ESCAPE ROOM THERAPY	135
CHAPTER 15.	JESSICA BOTERO EKHOFF, ESQ.	143
CHAPTER 16.	ARE YOU THERE, GOD?	157
CHAPTER 17.	HOMECOMING	167
	EPILOGUE	175
	ACKNOWLEDGMENTS	185

AUTHOR'S NOTE

Conversations about postpartum depression have become mainstream in recent years, but what about the postpartum mental health challenges no one talks about? What about when giving birth leads to delusions, rage, paranoia, and a whole range of other symptoms none of the baby books warn you about?

I wrote this book because I wanted to share my experience with postpartum-onset bipolar I disorder, mania, and psychosis: rare—and even more rarely discussed—complications of having a baby.

Experiencing extreme mental health struggles during what was supposed to be a joyful time was incredibly isolating. I desperately searched for firsthand accounts from other mothers who had gone through what I was going through and survived, but I found almost nothing. After I fully recovered, I knew I had to share the story I wish I could have read during the hardest, loneliest time in my life.

My hope is that, in reading this book, you will gain a broader understanding of the full range of ways in which mental health can be affected by having a baby. I hope you come away with an extra layer of empathy for the new mothers in your life. If you have experienced your own battle with bipolar disorder, mania, or psychosis, I hope you feel seen and understood. Most importantly, I hope you realize there is a path to recovery. Brighter days will come for you, just as they came for me.

CHAPTER 1

WAITING FOR WELLS

I had been worried about the snow all week. It was February in Chicago, and with Wells due to come any day, I was having nightmares about our tiny Mazda getting stuck in a snowdrift while I was in labor. It wasn't out of the realm of possibility. Just the week before, on my way to an obstetrician appointment, the car's wheels became lodged in the sludge outside our garage, and it took Dane and an irritated, blocked-in neighbor to dig them out. Our friends Kyle and Katie, with their brand-new SUV, were already on standby and ready to drive us to the hospital if needed. But the idea of soaking their Volvo's leather seats with amniotic fluid was less than appealing.

Drumming my fingers on my baby-stretched belly, I wandered into the nursery to check the hospital bag again. Starting maternity leave a few days before my due date was supposed to give me time to decompress, but mostly I just felt fidgety and impatient. A person can only cook so many freezer meals.

I unzipped the duffel bag and rifled through its contents. I checked to make sure I'd packed the twinkle lights our doula had suggested to make the delivery room cozier. Assessing the snack supply, I added a few more granola bars. I didn't want to get hungry during labor. I pulled out Wells's going-home outfit, a footed onesie covered with blue and green hearts, and tried to imagine the outfit filled out with a warm, squirming body, but couldn't. Bringing home a baby was going to be entirely uncharted territory for me. As an only child who skipped over the high school babysitting phase, at thirty-four I'd never changed a diaper or fed a bottle.

To make up for my lack of real-world experience, I read every pregnancy and newborn book I could get my hands on. I could rattle off "the five S's" of sleep without skipping a beat and was well versed in the debates on pacifier use and feeding schedules. I knew about all Wells's developments and which vegetable size he could be compared to in any given week of gestation.

I had bristled at the judgmental tone surrounding formula. Baby book writers seemed to view women as milk factories and didn't place any value on our desire to reclaim our bodies after nine long months. I didn't like the thought of being the person exclusively responsible for feeding Wells, and the idea of tethering myself to a pump multiple times a day once I went back to work exhausted me.

I wanted Dane and I to be on equal footing when it came to Wells. Our marriage had always been one of equals, and I didn't want parenthood to change that. Ours was a household where we each did our own laundry and took turns cooking and cleaning the kitchen. We had already created a chart divvying up the new responsibilities Wells would bring into our lives—Dane in charge of arranging childcare, me in charge of doctors' visits. I didn't want all our carefully nurtured equality to fall by the wayside because Wells's constant feedings fell exclusively to me.

Tucking Wells's onesie back into the bag, I settled myself into the glider. I looked around the room, which had been ready for Wells's arrival for weeks. The accent wall with geometric shapes Dane had carefully created with painter's tape. The corner shelves loaded with colorful board books. The soft, speckled rug. The stuffed penguin propped up on the crib's railing. I was not especially skilled with home decor, but I loved how this calm, cozy space had come together.

I heard a "Tahoot!" from the living room. Dane was done with work for the day. "Tahoot" was one of his family traditions. Whenever his mom wanted to round the kids up, she'd call out, "Tahoot!" and they'd come running like ducklings. It had become a tradition in our house too.

Dane's job as a creative director at a large advertising agency meant he worked long, often erratic, hours. He was sometimes gone for a week at a time on commercial shoots. He recently went to Ghana to film an ad for a mosquito repellent company. The company took family portraits outside of churches and markets and printed the photos on special repellent-infused paper to be hung in people's living rooms. The goal was to protect homes from mosquitos using something attractive enough for people to actually use. I was proud of Dane's creativity and all the unique ideas he came up with, even if his good work often meant he received even more of it and was extra busy as a result.

I heaved my swollen body out of the glider, glancing down at what had formerly been my ankles but were now just extensions of my calves, running to my feet with barely a bump where the bones should be. My body seemed almost allergic to pregnancy, starting to puff up right from the beginning. With my due date almost here, I'd managed to pack over fifty pounds onto my five foot, three inch frame. My mother repeatedly asked me why my obstetrician was letting me get "so big." My knees protested when I climbed the stairs, and my back ached if I didn't change positions often enough. Dane, who normally detested feet, felt bad enough for me that I got a foot rub most nights.

The fact that Dane set aside his aversion to feet wasn't all that surprising. He was the kindest person I knew. Except for a college roommate who owned a smelly ferret he refused to bathe, Dane never spoke badly about anyone. He nurtured his friendships and gave everyone the benefit of the doubt. He never let a day go by without saying he loved me at least a few times. Our relationship was built on a foundation of warmth. I could count on one hand the number of times we'd had real fights over our fourteen years together. Raising our voices to each other was just not something we did. We valued open communication and prided ourselves on calmly talking through disagreements.

"There's my favorite preggo," Dane smiled at me as I waddled into the kitchen.

I draped my arms over his shoulders and sagged toward the floor with a dramatic sigh. "I love this baby more than life itself, but I also want to evict it."

Dane placed his hands on either side of my stomach and stage-whispered, "Don't take it personally. She probably says that about me too."

I giggled, then moved Dane's hand to where Wells had started to kick.

"This kid has some solid moves," Dane said approvingly.

"Indeed. Now, if he'd just move out of my uterus, all would be well with the world."

"He'll be out and about soon enough. He's got to be running out of room in there."

I rolled my eyes. "My body has demonstrated a limitless ability to expand. I don't think lack of space is going to be the thing that gets him out."

"Patience, young one. Go sit and I'll make us some dinner." Dane pulled two meal kits in brown paper bags out of the refrigerator. "What'll it be: lemon chicken Milanese or sweet potato rice bowl?"

"Chicken, please," I said, plopping down on the couch and grabbing my phone, ready to squeeze in some audiobook time while Dane cooked. The book I was listening to, *Big Summer*, was about a plus-sized fashion influencer who was unexpectedly invited to be in her long-lost best friend's wedding, where a murder ended up taking place. It was a fun, breezy read.

Thirty minutes later, we were sitting at the table with steaming plates of breaded chicken and lemon pasta in front of us.

"So, what kind of mischief did you get up to today?" Dane asked, spearing a piece of rotini.

"Nothing too crazy. I painted my nails. Then I read for a bit. I went through Wells's room and tried to think of anything we forgot to get him."

"And?" Dane raised an eyebrow.

"Nothing. The kid officially has everything any reasonable baby could ask for."

Dane laughed. "And to think, we didn't even have a registry! People get way too excited about buying baby stuff."

I shrugged. "Tiny things are always cuter."

And that's when I felt it. A dull cramp, like the first day of my period, crept across my belly.

Dane cocked his head at the expression on my face. "Everything okay?"

"Yeah, I just felt a weird cramp." I grimaced and rubbed my hand across the bottom of my belly, where it rested on my thighs. "Probably just the warm-up for what's coming."

We went back to our dinner but, a few minutes later, I felt another cramp.

"Do you think this is it?" Dane asked, his voice a mixture of excitement and nerves.

"Maybe? But my water hasn't even broken."

"Most women don't have their water break before they get to the hospital," Dane pointed out. He had paid even better attention to our childbirth classes than I had. We had taken an extensive eight-week session offered by our doula, where every week we logged onto Zoom for two hours to discuss advocating for ourselves in the hospital, using pressure point massage to manage labor pain, and the risks and benefits of induction and home birth. We even got homework, which Dane made sure we completed every week. He always asked more questions than the other dads in the class and took careful notes in the workbook our doula gave us. I knew he would be as ready as possible when the time came.

Another cramp hit me, this one a bit more forceful than the last. "Let's start timing them to see if they're regular," I said.

Dane opened the contraction timer app on his phone.

As the hours passed, my contractions grew stronger and closer together. I tried to watch an episode of my go-to comfort show, *Gilmore Girls*, but I was in too much pain to focus. Dane drew me a warm bath, and I sank into the water, writhing each time a fresh contraction hit. I forced myself to focus on my breathing. Like in yoga class, in through my nose and out through my mouth. The last thing I needed was to hyperventilate. Finally, around 1:00 a.m., the pain became unbearable.

"It's time to go to the hospital," I declared. "Mama needs an epidural."

"Let's do it," Dane said, hitching my hospital bag over his shoulder. He helped me put on my snow boots, then called our doula to let her know we were headed to the hospital. She agreed to meet us on the labor and delivery floor.

I tugged the zipper of my maternity coat over my bump for the last time. I wouldn't miss the days of squeezing myself into the coat as it grew progressively tighter around my middle. Maternity sizing was no match for what felt like my record-setting weight gain.

Mercifully, Dane was able to get the car out of the garage without issue and pull it around to the front of our condo. Before I made my way outside, I took one final look around our living room. A DockATot and bouncer sat on the rug next to a wicker basket full of toys. A baby blanket draped over the back of the sofa. The next time I was in this room, I'd be a mother. In fact, every single time I'd ever set foot in this room again, I'd do so as a mother. I smiled and hugged myself at the thought, then took a deep breath and stepped outside.

A blast of February air pummeled my face, and I inhaled sharply. I began taking tentative steps down the walkway, terrified of slipping on the ice. I made it to our front gate before a shock of pain doubled me over. I grasped the gate with one hand and my stomach with the other, panting with the exertion of trying to keep myself steady. Dane flipped the hazard lights on, despite the early morning hour, and came to guide me the rest of the way to our car. Our back seat was lined with crinkly pee pads, a hedge against soaking the upholstery if my water broke. Despite the pain, I chuckled a bit. There was something truly absurd about pregnancy.

We sped down the quiet Chicago streets toward the hospital. I groaned in the back seat and concentrated on not throwing up from the pain. I could feel chicken and pasta creeping upward toward my throat. Dane coached me through each of the contractions, reminding me to breathe and that Wells would be here before we knew it.

We pulled up in front of the hospital, skidding a bit on the slick drive. Dane ran around to my door and opened it for me. I heaved my legs out, then bent over as a contraction stabbed into my belly. The time between contractions had become less than two minutes, and I was exhausted from the near-constant pain.

We made it inside, and Dane went to the front desk to check us in while I peeled off my coat and hat. The waiting room was suffocatingly hot. The pain and heat combined to form a heavy blanket of nausea.

After what felt like an eternity, I was hoisted onto a gurney and shuttled upstairs to the labor and delivery floor. The anesthesiologist gave me the much-anticipated epidural, and my legs fell pleasantly numb. Released from the pain, I started to relax.

Our doula arrived and immediately set to work. She strung the twinkle lights and turned on one of the playlists Dane and I had made, a mix filled with mellow indie songs called "Preggos Wanna Chill." She got me a peanut ball to prop between my knees and gave me sips from a cup of cranberry-apple juice. I drifted off to sleep.

A few hours later, I hadn't made much progress. I was still six centimeters dilated, and my epidural was beginning to wear off. The anesthesiologist returned to administer another dose, leaving my legs like cement-filled logs.

My obstetrician, Dr. Morton, came in and frowned at the monitor. "The baby's heart rate is going down every time you have a contraction. We need to keep an eye on it."

I could feel my own heart rate starting to rise. I didn't like the sound of what Dr. Morton was saying.

A few tense hours later, it was time to push. Wells's heart rate was still dipping with each contraction, and Dr. Morton warned me I'd need a C-section if he didn't come soon. I'd been dreading the thought of a C-section since I became pregnant. The idea of caring for a newborn after major abdominal surgery sounded completely daunting. I planned to do everything in my power to avoid it.

As the room filled with medical residents, I pulled my thighs into my chest and pushed with everything I had. I thought about junior high track meets and what it felt like to give every last ounce of effort right before reaching the finish line. And then I heard a tiny cry and saw Dane's shining eyes.

"He's here!" Dane exclaimed. Dane's tears fell onto my temple as he kissed my sweaty cheek. Dr. Morton handed Wells to me, and he immediately nuzzled into my chest. I couldn't believe he was here. My very own little person. Someone to take to swimming classes, to make laugh, and to cuddle with on lazy Sunday mornings. Dane and I had spent the last several months talking about the next chapter of our lives, and now that chapter was finally here.

CHAPTER 2

CAREER COACH

We got lucky with the recovery room. Normally it was reserved for families with twins, but because there were none that day, we got the corner room with extra space and a view of Lake Michigan, sparkling in the cold. Wells dozed in the see-through bassinet next to my bed while Dane and I gazed at him, stunned at the knowledge that he was real and he was ours.

Our time in the recovery room passed in a blur of fragmented sleep, interrupted by Wells's hungry cries and a rotating assortment of doctors and nurses stopping by to check vitals, test Wells's hearing, and see if I needed any more supplies. We learned how to swaddle Wells and feed him with a syringe. We watched in delight as Wells received his first bath and giggled like children when he peed on the nurse trying to clean his squirming body.

On our last day in the recovery unit, a new-parent nurse-educator named Angela came to our room. She talked about handling the stresses of the first few weeks home with Wells, the importance of sleep, and postpartum depression symptoms to watch out for. I had read several books that discussed postpartum mental health and felt ready to address anything that might come up. I'd been in therapy at several points throughout my life and always found it useful. I had no qualms about asking for help. Although I felt I already knew everything there was to know on the topic, I listened politely as Angela went through her talking points. Then she asked about my experience using a doula.

"I'd recommend it to anyone," I said. "I thought it was going to be too granola for me, but I ended up loving it. It was great having someone in the room whose sole purpose was to look out for me and lead me through the whole process. The nurses were great, but they had other patients, and it was nice being able to ask all my questions right away. Plus, she hung twinkle lights in the delivery room."

Angela's eyes lit up. "I love hearing stories like that. I'm going to tell you something. I love what I do, honest to God. But I'm not sure it's my calling anymore. Lately, I've been thinking about getting my certification and becoming a doula myself."

"You should do it!" I enthused. "Having a nursing background would be a huge asset. It's every pregnant lady's dream to have a nurse at her beck and call the entire time she's in labor. You'd have more clients than you'd know what to do with."

"I'd love to give it a try, but it scares me too. I'm fifty-four years old. That's not when most people start a new career." Angela gave a little self-deprecating laugh.

"That doesn't matter," I said, shaking my head. "I think it's brave to start over when you've been doing the same thing for a long time. It's easy to settle and just do what you've always done. Most people wouldn't be willing to take the risk."

"You know, I think I'd be good at it," Angela said, a cautious smile pulling at the corners of her lips. "I just need to figure out how to make it happen."

"You should talk to my doula! I'm sure she'd be happy to give you advice on how to get started. She used to be a nurse too. And she's super nice."

"Really?" asked Angela, raising her eyebrows. "It'd be great to have someone give me some pointers. This would be such a big change for me."

Wells had woken up and started to fuss. Dane kept trying to catch my eye, and I could tell he wanted me to wrap up my conversation so I could nurse, but I was getting excited picturing a new life for Angela.

"You should absolutely talk to my doula," I repeated. "She's been doing it for years and would have a ton of good advice. Maybe she could even be your mentor!"

I was getting more and more fired up about the idea. What if this was the conversation that gave Angela the push she needed to follow her passion? People come into one another's lives for a reason, and maybe I had been put in Angela's path to help her embrace her true purpose.

It could be like the time I volunteered as a tutor. Every Tuesday, I met my assigned student, Ayana, in a run-down grade school classroom and helped her with her fourth-grade math problems and spelling words. I wanted to make a real difference, so I took things one step further. I went to a teachers' supply store and bought multiplication flash cards and a wheel for teaching fractions. I also bought a series of books with main characters who looked like Ayana and had big professional dreams, like becoming scientists or ballerinas. I wrote her a note every week that she was supposed to save and only open on Saturday. The notes gave her little challenges, like asking her grandmother to tell her a story about what her own childhood had been like. I spent a lot of time thinking about what to put in those notes. Over the weeks, Ayana started opening up to me, and I could tell she looked forward to our Tuesday afternoons together. I had made a difference in her life, and now I wanted to do the same for Angela.

By this point, Wells had started to wail, and Angela excused herself to go see her next patient. But I couldn't stop thinking about her as I unzipped my sweatshirt and settled Wells against my chest. What could I do to help her on her path to becoming a doula? Maybe I could buy her a book about career change and send it to her office. Or maybe I could call her boss and tell her Angela had done such a good job explaining what to expect in new parenthood that she deserved a raise. A raise could help her save money for her doula classes. I wondered whether she could take the classes at night or on the weekends or if she would need to quit her job. I wondered how long a doula class lasted.

"Babe, I think he's done," Dane said, interrupting my train of thought.

I glanced down and saw Wells had fallen asleep. I hadn't noticed the sucking sensation had stopped.

"What do you think I can do to help Angela become a doula?" I asked.

Dane gave me a strange look. "I think Angela can figure that out for herself. I don't think she needs your help."

But I knew he was wrong. Something told me that Angela very much did need me, and I wasn't going to let her down.

*****

"What's up next, La Lecheria or The Rootery?" I asked, marker in hand. We had given my breasts restaurant names to amuse ourselves during the never-ending feeding sessions and to remind ourselves which side each feeding should start on. We kept track of this, along with Wells's sleep and wake periods, on a dry-erase board in the nursery. We brought Wells home from the hospital the day before and were settling into our new life as a family of three.

"Table for one at The Rootery," Dane replied, settling into the chair next to my nursing glider.

I scooped Wells out of his bassinet and eased into the glider, arranging myself carefully amidst the postpartum soreness. As I sat, I could hear the squelch of the ice pad lining my underwear. Wells started whimpering, and I helped position his mouth on my right breast. Soon he quieted and began sucking rhythmically.

"Ready to puzzle?" asked Dane.

"Always."

At the beginning of the pandemic, we had gotten into crossword puzzles. It started with a few minutes a day spent doing the mini crossword on the *New York Times* app, then moved on to the real thing. At first, we could only handle Monday puzzles, the week's easiest. But, over time, we worked our way to the more challenging Wednesday puzzles, which we printed from the online archive and completed together every Sunday morning.

"Okay, 1 Across," read Dane. "Yoko ____."

"Again? I swear, they're obsessed with Yoko Ono. We've had her as a clue at least three times."

"Total fanboys. But at least we've got a good start on our upper left corner." Dane filled in the squares and moved on to the next clue.

We stayed like that for the next half hour, Dane reading the clues and me craning my neck from the glider to see which squares remained blank. I felt proud of us. I was confident the vast majority of parents to four-day-old babies didn't complete *New York Times* crossword puzzles. But we were committed to maintaining the parts of ourselves that made us who we were before Wells arrived. I was still going to watch all the major international figure skating competitions. Dane would get back into the pottery studio as soon as pandemic restrictions eased. And we would keep doing the crossword puzzle every week, as had become our tradition.

We finished the puzzle, and a pleasurable wave of accomplishment washed over me. Only four days in and we were already nailing this parenting thing. It wouldn't be as hard as people said.

Dane announced he was going to take a nap before the next feeding and asked if I wanted to join him, but I declined. I needed to work on my plan to help Angela. I knew she was counting on me, even though she hadn't said as much, and I wanted to see her succeed. I could picture myself at a graduation ceremony for Angela's doula certification class. Would she be allowed to give a speech, and would she thank me by name? Maybe I could take her out for lunch afterward. I'd invite her family too, of course. It would be my treat. I thought about what kind of restaurant would be appropriate. I wanted it to be someplace suitably celebratory, but not too over-the-top. I didn't want Angela to think I was showing off.

But I was getting ahead of myself. First, I had to make sure Angela met my doula, Heather, who could shepherd her through the certification process. The only problem was I didn't have Angela's contact information. I had given Heather's email address to Angela when we talked in my hospital room, but I couldn't guarantee Angela would reach out to her. People are often hesitant to ask for help. I wanted to introduce Angela and Heather by email to get the conversation started.

I decided to call the labor and delivery ward. I told the nurse who answered that I had spoken to Angela right before my discharge and had a follow-up question. The nurse asked if it was anything she could help with, but I said I already felt comfortable with Angela and wanted to discuss my issue with her. The nurse checked the schedule, but Angela wasn't working that day. I asked when she'd be in next, and the nurse put me on hold while she checked.

This was taking longer than expected, but I was committed. I had hoped to get some sleep after I sorted everything out with Angela, but I might have to wait until Wells's next nap. No big deal, I thought. I was surprisingly energized, despite having slept only a few hours in the last four days. I had too many things on my mind. As soon as I lay down, my brain started making lists and planning what to do with my free time during Wells's next nap.

And that was when I lay down at all. One of my biggest fears about motherhood was losing myself along the way. I didn't want to be one of those women who tied their entire identity to parenting. I was desperate to keep reading, making time for phone calls with friends, and baking. I wanted to keep being myself, just with my new role as a mother mixed in. So when Wells and Dane lay down to sleep, I often picked up a book or rifled through my recipe collection. There were only so many hours in the day and, besides, I was finding I needed less sleep than expected.

The nurse came back on the line and told me Angela was scheduled to be back on Thursday. Today was Monday. Not soon enough. Angela had a dream, and she might lose momentum if she didn't act now. I couldn't let that happen.

I asked the nurse whether she had a phone number for Angela. She didn't, but said I could check with the hospital education department. She gave me the number to the department, but I must have written it down wrong because when I called, I reached cardiology. No matter, I thought. I called the hospital's main line and asked for the education department. I was put on hold for what seemed like an eternity, then finally put through. But the woman who answered didn't have Angela's phone number either. I was becoming increasingly frustrated, but I refused to be deterred.

I checked the baby monitor. Wells was sleeping soundly in his bassinet, wrapped tightly in his giraffe-print swaddle. I wasn't tired, so I had more time to think about how to contact Angela. Suddenly, I had an idea. My friend Katie was a doctor at the hospital, and my friend Jess was a nurse. I texted them and asked what the email syntax for the hospital was so I could make an educated guess about Angela's email address. After Katie responded, I wrote a long, heartfelt email to my doula, telling her all about Angela, how kind she had been to me in the hospital, and how I was certain she'd make an excellent doula if she had someone to show her the ropes. I copied Angela on the email, then closed my laptop with a satisfied sigh. It felt good to change a life.

CHAPTER 3

JAUNDICE

―

After Dane woke up from his nap, we decided it was time to call the pediatrician. During the past few days, we'd gotten a historic amount of snow. Rippling, knee-high layers blanketed the sidewalks and piled into a mound in front of our gate. The cars parked on the street outside our building looked like indistinct blobs of shimmering white. The temperature had barely crept into the double digits, and icy gusts of wind ripped through the air. There was no way we were going to take Wells out for his four-day appointment in this weather.

Before Dane called the pediatrician to reschedule the appointment, I told him we should practice what he was going to say. "They're going to pressure you," I warned him. "It's their policy to have babies come in on day four, and they're going to try to convince you to get there. Don't give in. We're not going." My voice came out fiercer than I had intended.

"I get it," Dane said, putting a hand on my shoulder. "We're on the same page. You don't need to get upset." Dane dialed our pediatrician and turned on the speakerphone so I could hear the conversation.

We had decided Dane would call because he was calmer than me. Over the past day, as the snow continued piling up outside our windows and the temperature plummeted, I became increasingly concerned about the four-day visit. I didn't feel safe out on the roads with tiny Wells in this weather, especially in our little Mazda. But I felt certain the doctor's office was going to try to bully us into keeping the appointment on the scheduled date.

The receptionist transferred us to a nurse who, predictably, insisted we come in that afternoon.

"It's important for the jaundice test to be given on the fourth day because that's when bilirubin levels peak," the nurse said.

"I understand that, and I know it would be ideal if we came in today, but we just don't feel safe," Dane explained.

"We really do recommend coming in on baby's fourth day. Jaundice can be a very serious condition. It can lead to brain damage if left untreated."

I could feel my cheeks beginning to heat.

"He doesn't have jaundice," I insisted, leaning over Dane's shoulder to get closer to the phone. "He's eating fine, and his skin doesn't look even a little bit yellow."

Dane shushed me.

"Jaundice can't be assessed just by looking at the skin. We need to check the baby's liver levels," said the nurse. "Is there anyone who could drive you into the office today?"

A swell of anger rose in my chest. "We already told you, we don't feel safe taking Wells out on the roads. It doesn't matter who drives us. We're not bringing a four-day-old out in two-degree weather. The roads are all ice."

This is what was wrong with the American health care system, I thought. No common sense and no empathy. Who did this woman think she was? I gave birth four days ago, in the middle of a pandemic, no less, and she had the gall to try to intimidate me and make me question my competence as a mother? I was a good parent, I assured myself. Just because I didn't want to risk all our safety for some four-day test didn't make me bad at caring for Wells.

"I would say that the risks of unchecked jaundice are serious enough to warrant finding a way to come into the office today, even if the driving conditions aren't the best. All our office employees were able to make it in safely today," the nurse continued.

I felt myself gearing up for a fight. It was like handling a settlement negotiation where opposing counsel was using bullying tactics, or taking a deposition where the defending attorney insisted on interrupting with bogus objections. I thought back to the time when, working on one of my longest-running cases several years ago, opposing counsel and I got into an argument over a missed conference call. The other lawyer sent me a condescending email saying, "I don't know who you think you're talking to, but I don't take instructions from associates." I had been practicing law for five years at the time and was livid. I insisted to my boss that a response was called for and crafted a perfectly worded email telling the other lawyer that, in response to his question about who I thought I was talking to, the answer was a professional equal with the same license to practice law he had. Sending that email made me feel so powerful. I sensed that desire for power coming to the surface again. I was glad being a litigator had prepared me for situations like this.

"Today isn't an option," I announced firmly. "What's Dr. Jackson's availability tomorrow?"

The nurse sighed. "I understand you're worried about the roads, and everything feels more consequential as a new parent. But I really have to insist—"

I shook my head emphatically and cut her off. "You're not listening to me. I've told you repeatedly we're not coming in today. I don't know how I could be more clear." My voice was rising, and Dane was making the universal "calm down" sign at me.

I ignored him.

"There's nothing you can say that will make me change my mind. We're not coming in today, and that's the end of it. Now, will you just tell me when Dr. Jackson is free tomorrow? Otherwise, we're not coming in then either."

I should have just handled the call from the beginning. Dane was too soft. He would have let this woman walk all over us if I hadn't intervened.

"I'll just say one last time that refusing to come in today is against the doctor's recommendations, but, if you insist, I'll go check his calendar for tomorrow."

"Thank you," I said, in a tone indicating I was anything other than grateful. I crossed my arms and gave a satisfied smile. I loved the feeling of victory.

CHAPTER 4

RAGE

We were in the nursery the next day when the smoke alarm went off. Dane was boiling Wells's new pacifiers to sanitize them, as our baby book had recommended, but had then gotten distracted when Wells started crying. We rushed into the hallway and were confronted with the noxious smell of burning plastic. It was like someone had tried to create a bonfire out of a pile of Barbie dolls. I clamped my hand over Wells's nose and mouth.

"Shit!" Dane yelled, running to turn off the stove and grabbing the pot of water. "I'll take this outside, you take Wells downstairs away from the fumes."

I hustled a screaming Wells down the stairs and shut us in Dane's office. My mind was racing. How long had Wells been exposed to those fumes? Ten seconds? Thirty? It wasn't long, but, for such a young brain, could it be enough to cause long-term damage? Dane would never forgive himself, and I would struggle to curb my blame.

Wells's shrieks reverberated in my ear. I began marching around Dane's office, bouncing Wells in my arms with each step. His cries became a bit less frantic. I remembered what our baby book said about shushing sounds, and how they had to be right next to a baby's ear and louder than their crying to be effective. I added the shushing to my marching, emitting a crisp, loud shush with every step. I breathed in between shushes so as not to break the rhythm. Wells's shrieks melted into whimpers.

The shushing breath reminded me of my years in concert band, where I was an oboe player. We learned how to take quick breaths in between notes to avoid interrupting the song. It was that breath I used now, shuttling Wells back and forth across the carpet with measured, decisive steps.

Maybe I could write a blog post about this experience—"What Concert Band Taught Me about Parenthood." Maybe I could create a whole collection of blog posts about parenthood. They could be structured as a series of lessons about parenting learned from other areas of my life. I began to brainstorm. I thought about how I'd held my ground against the pediatrician's nurse and decided "What Being a Litigator Taught Me about Parenthood" could be another post in the series.

Another post could be "What Improv Comedy Taught Me about Parenthood." I started taking improv classes six years ago, a few years into my legal practice. I didn't want my career to completely consume me. I wanted to remain a whole person with hobbies and interests outside of work. And I wanted to do something that was purely for myself.

I had been interested in improv since college, when I used to watch the university's troupe on Wednesday nights in the student union. I was always so impressed by their performances; they were quick, and outlandish, and clever, and never seemed to be at a loss for words. It was like a superpower. There was only one woman on the team, Lauren, who later became an on-air media personality. The scenes with Lauren in them were always my favorites. I loved how she stood her ground and didn't let all the men outshine her. Improv, like many worlds, is male dominated. I had written for the college's satire newspaper and considered myself funnier than average, but I never had the nerve to audition for the improv team. Lauren was braver than me.

When I finally started taking improv classes, they made me feel self-conscious. I blushed every time my class played a goofy game like the famous Zip, Zap, Zop, where you slap your hands together and pass an imaginary ball around the circle. I was used to being seen as a professional, and being silly felt uncomfortable to me. It was a side of myself I had always been too buttoned-up to explore.

Over time, I learned improv wasn't about silliness but rather a hyperattentive type of listening that allowed you to understand the type of character your scene-mate was building and how to respond to them. It was about reacting from your gut without letting your head get in the way. It was about genuinely connecting with other people. There was something intoxicating about building a fictional world with another person, knowing that exact world would exist only for a few minutes and then never be built again. Improv scenes don't get repeated, and they don't get written down. They exist purely in the present and are only experienced by the people in the room. I relished the chance to be a part of it.

After a few years, I found myself in the same improv class as one of my former law school professors. Seeing him in baggy cargo pants and a waffle-knit shirt playing icebreaker games reminded me of the jolt I got when I ran into my second-grade teacher at the grocery store and realized she had a whole life outside of the classroom. I was impressed that this accomplished professor was willing to humble himself enough to be on the other side of the student/teacher divide. It's hard to be open to that level of vulnerability.

After our class was over, he invited me to join an improv team he was creating. The team consisted entirely of University of Chicago alums and was named after a former university president. We performed every month at The Revival, a new comedy club that had opened near campus. Performing with the team was like nothing I had ever done before. I loved our nerdy, witty brand of humor and the accolades we got from the comparably nerdy, witty audience members, most of whom were also affiliated with U of C. Nothing made them laugh harder than scenes about economic theories or the minutiae of local politics. I could feel my brain stretching with each performance.

By that point, Dane had started taking improv classes too, and would sometimes step in to perform with my team. He and I even talked about forming our own two-person team. Several venues around the city hosted time slots for independent improv teams, and we'd considered giving them a try. But then the pandemic hit, we had Wells, and improv fell by the wayside. That is, until we resurrected it somewhere around 2:00 a.m. when we discovered that making up characters and putting on terrible accents was the ideal way to pass the time while Wells fed.

Dane came into his office, interrupting my thoughts. He was pale, and his eyes looked strained. "I opened all the windows, but you can still smell the plastic. I think we should stay down here tonight."

We had a guest room on our lower level with its own bathroom. We could make it like indoor camping.

"I've got to go back up to get some supplies, but I wanted to check on you guys first. I'm glad he calmed down," Dane said, cupping his hand around the back of Wells's tender head.

Dane left and returned with Wells's bassinet, pajamas, and the makings of peanut butter and jelly sandwiches for dinner. After we'd eaten, I decided to investigate the status of the plastic fumes. I climbed the stairs and cautiously removed the mask I'd placed over my nose and mouth. I took a few tentative inhalations and relaxed. The plastic smell was gone.

I decided to take advantage of the quiet time to get a few chores done. I prepped freezer bags for breast milk and threw a load of Well's tiny clothes into the washer. I had just started to work on a grocery list when Dane poked his head up from the stairwell.

"It's been two hours, and Wells is starting to grumble. We should feed him soon."

I sighed. Apparently, I couldn't claim even ten minutes for myself without being expected to return to my mothering duties.

Breastfeeding had been a fraught topic for me. Throughout my pregnancy, the idea of it hadn't held much of an appeal. It seemed invasive, uncomfortable, and all-consuming. I had heard horror stories about weak latches, bloody nipples, and precious sleep time sacrificed to pump and increase supply. Whole Facebook groups were dedicated to swapping tips and offering commiseration (and a hearty dose of judgment). I joined an alternative group called Fed is Best.

My feminist side bristled at the idea of breastfeeding too. It drove me crazy to hear people say breastfeeding is free, which is true only if you believe women's time has no value. The idea that choosing not to breastfeed was selfish rankled me. I had done the research and felt breastfeeding didn't carry as many benefits as some people claimed. I also learned that much of the negativity surrounding formula stemmed from a 1970s debacle in which Nestlé was accused of selling formula in developing countries without proper instructions. Children died as a result, and formula's reputation was permanently tarnished.

It seemed to me the only reason reasteeding was pushed on new mothers with such ferocity was that society didn't value women's bodily autonomy and had no qualms about demanding they sacrifice themselves entirely for their children. For a long stretch of my pregnancy, I told Dane I didn't want to try breastfeeding at all. This had resulted in the closest we got to a fight, when Dane questioned whether it would be better for Wells if I did. I accused him of repeating platitudes without doing the research to back them up, and he quickly backed down.

But in the end, surprising myself more than anyone, I decided to give breastfeeding a try. I reasoned I would only have one chance in my life to try it, and I'd never know if I'd enjoy it unless I gave it a shot. My decision came with the condition that we wouldn't exclusively breastfeed Wells. I didn't want to be his sole source of nourishment, and I didn't want to feel like my body had become nothing more than a milk dispenser. So why was Dane pushing breastfeeding on me now?

"When you say 'we' should feed him, what you really mean is I should feed him, right?" I huffed. "I'm a woman, so every single feeding is my responsibility, no matter what else I have going on, and I should just shut my mouth and stop complaining about it, huh? I should just be the pretty little princess who sits quietly and does whatever the big boys say?"

Dane looked baffled. "What are you talking about?"

His response, which I interpreted as feigned ignorance, just made me madder. "I'm good for more than just feeding, you know. I'm not a cow. I'm a lawyer. And a fucking good one. Remember how I won an appellate argument when I was six months pregnant? You don't pull that off by being bad at what you do."

Dane had moved from baffled to concerned. "I'm not following. I never said you were a bad lawyer. And what does this have to do with feeding Wells?"

I exploded.

"It's easy for you to just stand there and pass judgments. Nobody expects anything of you. You can just take Wells out for a single stroller walk and everyone acts like you're the goddamn father of the year. All you have to do is *think* about changing a diaper and you get applauded. You have it so insanely easy, and you have the nerve to stand there and demand that I breastfeed on demand just because you snapped your fingers and said so?"

I could feel a storm of hot anger roiling in my chest. It felt uncontrollable but also invigorating. I had never yelled like this before. I was on a roll and wanted to keep going. I moved toward the stairs where Dane was standing, and he took a tentative step backward.

"What, you're scared of me now? Scared of a woman with opinions and a mouth she's not afraid to use?" I glared at Dane.

Dane's eyes were wide. "Stop yelling," he said insistently. "The neighbors are going to hear you."

"Oh yes, the neighbors. God forbid they hear me raising my voice and know you're not the only one who gets to talk in this house. Well, guess what? I get to talk too. I get to say—"

"Jessica, you need to calm down." Dane's voice was shaking.

I could feel my heart pounding hard in my chest. "Don't interrupt me! Don't you dare fucking interrupt me! Who do you think I am?" I stormed down the stairs with Dane backpedaling in front of me. "I'm so sick and tired of men thinking they get to interrupt me. Fuck Trump and all his fucking minions who think they get to trounce all over women. They don't, and neither do you!"

I heard Wells wailing in the guest room and saw Dane look over. I didn't want Dane to leave to go tend to him just as I was getting started. Our conversation was making me feel powerful, and I relished the sensation.

"I don't know what's going on right now, but we really need to feed him," Dane said cautiously. "Do you want to breastfeed him or should I go make a bottle?"

"Don't pretend like you think that's a real choice," I raged. "I know what you're thinking. You're thinking, 'She better breastfeed, or else she's a shit mother.' That's what you think, isn't it? You think my value to Wells is entirely wrapped up In my boobs? You think I can't be a good mother to him if I dare to feed him a bottle? What, are you going to call DCFS on me if I do?"

I cut myself short. What if Dane really was planning to call DCFS? What if he thought I was entirely incompetent and couldn't be trusted to take care of Wells? He was a man, and if he called the authorities and reported me, surely they'd believe him. Men were always believed over women. I knew that.

"Don't you *dare* call DCFS on me," I hissed. "I mean it. If you do, I swear I'll make you regret it. I'm a lawyer. I know all the right people, and there's no way you're going to get my baby taken away from me."

With that, I turned on my heel and marched back up the stairs, leaving a screaming Wells behind.

CHAPTER 5

BRINGING IN THE REINFORCEMENTS

―

I had a vague notion that perhaps I had been rude to Dane earlier in the night and owed him an apology, but my brain couldn't pinpoint what I'd said or done. While I was doing the dishes, I felt a strange fog come over me, and my mind went blank. Unable to think properly, I couldn't remember what I had been doing before I pulled out a new sponge and started scrubbing. I had never felt that type of sensation before, but I chalked it up to stress about the burning plastic fumes.

I turned off the faucet and went downstairs. Dane was tending to Wells, so I headed into the bathroom to take a shower. Dane had brought all our shower supplies down earlier in the night, but I noticed he'd forgotten to bring towels. I immediately got the idea to start an improv scene about a detective searching for a missing towel. I smiled at the thought. It would be fun to play out a scene together and ease some of the stress of the night. I went into the guest room, where Dane was holding Wells, with my brow furrowed and my hands clasped behind my back, doing my best Sherlock Holmes impression.

"When I first got put on this case, it started out like any other night," I began, pacing the room slowly. Dane's eyes widened and I saw what I thought, strangely, was fear. "It's not like it was the first time I'd been called in for a missing towel, after all. These cases are a dime a dozen."

"Jessica, what are you talking about?" Dane's voice was low and shaky. I was surprised he hadn't caught on yet that we were improvising. Dane and I made up improv scenes all the time, and we were both good at picking up on the cues that a scene had begun.

"There were a number of suspects, but I decided to start with the husband. In my line of work, there's always a good chance it's the husband." I stroked my imaginary beard.

I saw Dane's hold on Wells tighten protectively. Wells started to whimper. "Please stop this. Whatever is going on right now, please just stop." Dane's voice trembled, and I saw, with a start, the beginnings of tears forming in his eyes.

I immediately realized my mistake. Dane was so stressed about having burned Wells's pacifiers and endangering him with the fumes that he couldn't loosen up enough to improvise with me. That had to be it. Dane was a sensitive person, and I was sure he must be feeling incredibly guilty about the accident.

I dropped my character. "Dane, I was just playing. It was supposed to be an improv scene. I saw you had forgotten to bring towels down, and I thought it would be fun to do a detective bit."

Relief washed over Dane's face. "Now isn't a good time for improv."

I nodded. "You're too stressed. I thought it would be fun, but it was bad timing."

Dane released a deep breath. "I think we need to call your parents."

Dane and I had decided while I was pregnant that we wanted to wait at least two weeks before our families came for visits. We wanted some time to acclimate to our new lives as a family of three. Plus, the idea of having to pick up the house and look presentable for visitors seemed daunting. But if Dane was feeling overwhelmed and wanted my parents' help, I wasn't going to say no.

"I'll call them in the morning," I said.

Dane shook his head. "I think we should call now. The sooner they can get here, the better."

I glanced at my watch. It was past 10:00 p.m. Dane must have been struggling even more than I realized. He was the calmest person I knew, so if he was this desperate for a few extra pairs of hands, he must be feeling entirely in over his head. I was surprised that parenthood was taking such a heavy toll on him, but I didn't want to judge. Besides, it would be nice to share the early days of Wells with my parents.

As an only child, I grew up having a close relationship with them. They drove me over an hour each way from our rural hometown for figure skating practice on Saturday mornings and never missed my volleyball games or band concerts. When I was young, before my social life took over my weekends, we'd rent a movie from the local video store and order a pizza from Monical's most Friday nights. It was the only time we ever ate in front of the TV. We always sat down for breakfast together before school, and whenever we traveled for vacation, it was just the three of us. Even when I angered them by talking back or sneaking out to meet friends for milk shakes at Steak 'n Shake, I knew they still loved me. I had always been the focal point of their lives. They were thrilled when I told them they were going to be grandparents, and I knew they would relish the opportunity to meet Wells earlier than expected.

I went into Dane's office to FaceTime them. Although it was late, I was sure they'd still be awake. Ever since I'd introduced them to Netflix a few years ago, they'd become addicted to binging shows late into the night. When they answered, they were both on-screen and looking mildly concerned.

"Hi J. Is everything okay over there?" my mom asked. She wasn't accustomed to receiving late-night calls from me.

"Well, I have some news I think you'll like," I said brightly. "I know we said we wanted to wait a few weeks before we had you visit, but we changed our minds and would love it if you could come now."

My mom raised her eyebrows. "Really? We'd be more than happy to. But what changed?"

I recounted the story of the burning pacifiers, rushing Wells out of the fumes, and Dane's struggle to handle all the stress.

"Dane doesn't mind us coming early?" my mom asked.

"He asked me to call you," I said.

My dad nodded. "Great. We'll pack a bag and be there first thing tomorrow morning."

Thinking about my parents meeting Wells suddenly gave me an idea. "While I have you, I've been wanting to talk about Grandpa."

My relationship with my grandfather had never been a good one. He rarely came to any of my sporting events or other activities growing up, even though he lived a few blocks from my school. He missed my sixteenth birthday party so he could play in a golf tournament. He never took much of an interest in anything about my life.

Despite these neglectful tendencies, he was ostentatiously religious, singing loudly in the choir on Sunday mornings and giving lectures on the importance of living a godly life. The hypocrisy grated on me, especially after I became an attorney and he took to bragging to anyone who would listen about his big-city lawyer granddaughter. This, despite his failure to do anything to help me get to where I was. He had stood idly by while I took on six figures of debt to attend law school and purchased a monstrous Mercedes SUV rather than helping me with my tuition. It wasn't as though I felt entitled to his wealth, but for someone with more money than he knew what to do with and a penchant for preaching about Christian values, it seemed like helping me would have been the right thing to do.

My grandfather had now reached his mid-eighties, and after a stroke left him with neuropathy in his hands and feet, his golf days were over. He still lived at home but had around-the-clock care from a series of nurses. The last time I had begrudgingly gone to visit him, he'd been unable to get out of his chair on his own. He had recently started using oxygen at night, and his care team didn't think he had much longer to live.

"Unless one of you wants me to, I'm not going to bring Wells to meet him," I told my parents. "I don't want to give him the satisfaction of bragging to all his friends about his great-grandson." I could feel a swell of righteous anger rising in my chest. It felt good.

"He doesn't deserve to meet Wells," I continued. "He was a shitty grandpa to me, and he'd be the same for Wells." My voice was beginning to rush out faster and faster. "I'm done having him in my life. And when he dies, I'm not going to his funeral."

I wasn't quite sure where that final declaration had come from, but it felt right. I wasn't going to shroud myself in black and pretend to mourn a man who had let me down time and time again throughout my life.

"Dad, is there any reason why you want me to take Wells to meet Grandpa? Because if you want me to, I'll do it, but if it's not important to you, then I won't. Which is it?" The words tumbled out of me, and I suddenly felt desperate to know his answer. I wanted the question to be resolved and the answer final so I could set it aside and move on.

"Jessica, this is really up to you. I'm not going to tell you—"

I shook my head vigorously and held my hand out in front of me, cutting him off. "I just want a yes or no. Is it important to you that I introduce Wells to Grandpa or not?" I was feeling restless and impatient. Why couldn't my father just answer the question? I'd made it so simple.

"Where is all of this coming from?" my dad asked. "Do you really want to talk about it right now?"

"Yes. I'm a parent now, and I don't have time to be wishy-washy about things anymore. I just want to knock this out. I want to make a decision and move on. I don't have time to go back and forth on this." I slapped my hand on the desk between each word for emphasis. "I. Don't. Have. Time."

My dad turned to my mom and gave her an uncomfortable look. He was like an animal who had been backed into a corner with no way out. "If you don't want to bring Wells to meet your grandfather, then there's no need to do it on my account."

I nodded briskly. "Good. That's all I needed to know. I'm glad that's settled."

My parents exchanged a glance.

"We're going to go get some sleep," my mom said. "We want to get on the road early tomorrow."

I nodded. "Thank you for doing this. I've never seen Dane so stressed. It's clear he really needs help."

The hours between when I called my parents and when they arrived are a blur in my memory. I know they involved Dane locking himself and Wells into our guest room to protect themselves from my rage. I also know that by the time my parents arrived, I was convinced Dane had called DCFS to take Wells away from me. I repeatedly lunged at his phone, demanding he unlock it and show me his call log. When Dane told me my parents had arrived and were outside, I was sure it was really the DCFS agents coming to save Wells from his incompetent mother. I threw myself to the ground in our living room so they couldn't see me through the windows and covered my face with a pillow.

When my mother walked through the front door, I began sobbing uncontrollably. She rushed to kneel at my side, and I buried my head in her lap like a toddler scared of a thunderstorm. I felt an immense rush of relief. My mother made everything better, safer. I remembered the comfort I always received from her as a child. I could confess any childhood misstep or mistake, confident in the knowledge that she would still love me. She always made me feel like my problems were manageable.

Curled on the ground with my mother running her fingers through my sweaty hair, I could feel my breath start to even out. Maybe Dane hadn't filed a DCFS complaint against me after all. Maybe I was a good mother to Wells, or at least good enough. Maybe I could sleep for the first time in the past few days. Maybe.

*****

I woke up after a fitful hour of sleep with a queasy feeling in my stomach. Something was wrong. I remembered finding myself curled on the ground in our living room with a pillow over my face the night before but couldn't recall why. I knew I had gotten irrationally angry at Dane and essentially stalked him down the stairs while yelling at him but, again, couldn't put my finger on my motive. I remembered the look of fear in his eyes when I tried to initiate the missing towel improv bit. He had almost looked scared of me.

I put on a robe and stumbled sleepily into the kitchen. Dane was making coffee and my parents were sitting at the kitchen table.

"There's my little angel," my mom said, rising from the table to hug me.

I sat down, and an uncomfortable silence fell over the kitchen. I saw Dane exchange a look with my parents he clearly hadn't intended for me to see.

Dane took a deep breath. "I think we need to talk about something."

"Okay," I said slowly. I glanced over at my parents. My mom was biting her lip, and my dad was clenching his hands on the tabletop. They were both looking at Dane expectantly.

"I think something's wrong," Dane said. "You haven't been yourself. You've been yelling, and you've been having a lot of—" he chose his words carefully, "strange thoughts. I'm not sure what's going on, but I think we need to get you help."

"Something does feel off," I admitted. "I can't put my finger on it, but I think I've been angry more than normal. And I feel scattered. Like I keep losing my train of thought, and I have these weird holes in my memory."

Dane looked relieved. "I'm glad you've realized it too. I was worried you'd put up a fight."

I could see a bit of color coming back into Dane's drained face.

"I've already talked to Alyssa," Dane went on. Alyssa was a good friend of ours and a social worker at a high school in the suburbs. "She knows about a special intensive outpatient therapy program for new moms."

I cocked my head. The word "intensive" threw me. "That sounds like a lot. I was just thinking I should find a new therapist."

Dane hesitated. "I think you need more than that."

I frowned. "Do you think I'm crazy or something? You realize I'm not crazy, right? I'm just a new mom who's under a lot of stress."

"No one thinks you're crazy," Dane rushed to say. "But the way you've been acting and what you've been saying are—" he paused to pick his words again, "different from what's normal for a new mom."

I sighed. "I'm not sure it's that big of a deal, but if it would make you feel better, I'll do it. As long as they don't try to lock me up or anything."

I had meant the last part as a weak attempt at a joke. I had zero expectation that anyone would think I needed to be hospitalized for yelling at my husband a bit too much and being a little scatterbrained. Wasn't that how every new mother felt? Of course, I had to admit I was finding it harder and harder to concentrate; hard enough that I had been leaving myself an increasing number of Post-it notes around the house to remember the basic tasks I needed to accomplish. And I wasn't able to sleep more than an hour or two at a time. I lay down with my mind racing and woke up with it pawing through a sea of new thoughts and ideas, struggling to decide which one to latch on to. But all that seemed normal to me. I had a brand-new baby; what did people expect of me? I was fine. Everything was going to be fine.

"I made an appointment on Saturday for you to do the intake for the program," said Dane. "It was the earliest opening they had. You should be able to start therapy on Monday."

I nodded. I had always been a big advocate of therapy. When I was a junior in high school, a girl who had been a close friend when I was younger died by suicide. There had been no red flags, as far as I could tell, and no note. Whitney had been the most popular girl in my class, with the perfect flipped-out hair and the perfect senior boyfriend. I had been one of the last people to talk to her before she died. I distinctly remember standing at our lockers at the end of the day, noting her St. Louis Cardinals shirt, and commenting that I had thought she was a Cubs fan. It was an innocuous comment, one I gave basically no thought to. But an hour later, Whitney was gone, and I'd never forget my conversation with her. Why hadn't I realized something was wrong? Was there anything I could have said that would have stopped her?

I developed crippling anxiety, which was originally misdiagnosed as a heart murmur. I didn't grow up in a place where mental health was discussed. Even my doctor failed to consider that the teenage girl with the dead friend might be suffering from something other than a physical ailment. After much too long, I finally ended up in therapy. It saved me. I felt like I was holding my breath all week in between sessions. My therapist's office was the only place where I felt I could get relief. It was the only place where I could take a deep breath. Slowly but surely, I started to feel like myself again. The panic attacks abated, my palms stopped sweating, and my heart rate slowed. I was forever grateful for what my therapist did for me. So if it would make Dane feel better for me to do some type of intensive therapy program, then I wasn't going to put up a fight about it. It seemed like overkill, but there were worse things in the world than too much therapy.

CHAPTER 6

UNRAVELING

I had never referred to *The Bachelor* franchise as my guilty pleasure. I wasn't guilty about watching it, nor did I think I should be. The shows existed purely for entertainment, and I was always entertained when I watched them. I loved the breezy escape from reality, the silly drama, and the over-the-top dates. I even loved the predictability and cheesiness. It was like a balm for the stressors of everyday life. A little brain break.

But that day, when I settled in to watch the latest episode of *The Bachelor*, which I had been eagerly awaiting, things were different. It was the season featuring Matt James, the historic first Black Bachelor. Much had been made of this fact, particularly given Bachelor Nation's history of racial casting disparities. Many of Matt's contestants were also women of color. One such woman, Serena, was selected for the one-on-one date in the episode. When the couple was informed the date activity would be a private tantric yoga class, Serena gave an uncomfortable laugh.

"She's literally putting us in sex-based yoga positions when we haven't reached that stage in our relationship yet," Serena said, looking straight into the camera. "This is not for me.

It's not something I would have chosen for our date today." As the date concluded, she said she had been in her head the entire time, just waiting for the experience to be over.

A tidal wave of rage rose within me. How dare ABC do this? It was more than just exploitative. Serena had expressed her discomfort with the date, yet the producers clearly pressured her into doing it anyway. This must be illegal. It was essentially assault. My brain whirled back to my first year of law school when I had taken a torts class. The class was all about the various kinds of trouble people could get themselves into. Assault, battery, negligence, intentional infliction of emotional distress. What exactly was ABC guilty of here? They had essentially coerced Matt into assaulting Serena. So maybe some sort of contributory liability? I felt like I was back in finals season, taking an issue spotter exam where my job was to identify every cause of action and assess its merits. There was a thorny puzzle of liability to be worked out, and I was going to solve it. ABC would pay for what they had done.

I opened my laptop and created a new Word document. My heart raced. Matt and Serena, two people of color on a historically whitewashed show, had been assaulted at the hands of ABC. I was going to make the station pay for what it had done. I began drafting a letter.

Almost immediately, I switched from a draft to an outline. My thoughts were too scattered. New ideas popped into my mind so quickly I struggled to capture them all. I could barely get through a sentence before I felt compelled to start a new one. I wanted to chase down each idea and pounce on it before it escaped. I let myself freely associate with bullet points and brackets for ideas that needed to be researched or fleshed out further. I decided I could organize everything into a coherent letter later when my mind felt clearer.

ABC is putting profits ahead of contestant safety.

Serena didn't give explicit consent.

ABC forced Matt to assault Serena via the tantric yoga date. [Research exact cause of action. Contributory liability? Assault and battery? Attempted rape?]

[What's the cause of action for what happened to Matt? He technically assaulted Serena, but he's a victim too. Consider this more.]

I'm a partner at a law firm. I know people and can easily get the word out about ABC's attack on its contestants of color.

[Should I send the letter on law firm stationery? Might make them take me more seriously. But would I need to run a conflict check at work first? Didn't we try to get ABC as a client recently? Double-check.]

Contact attorney general and recommend pressing charges.

FCC violation?

ABC must donate to the postpartum mental health intensive outpatient therapy program I'll be joining, or else I'll tell everyone about their assault. I'm not going to tell them how much they need to donate, but if they don't give enough, I'll tell everyone anyway. [Decide how much they need to donate to stop me from exposing them.] That will incentivize them to maximize their donation.

Do I need a publicist? A lawyer? A social media manager?

Do I know anyone who may know someone at ABC?

I thought about how I would spread the word if ABC failed to comply with my demands. I could contact former contestants and have them join me in speaking out. I bet Becca Kufrin, a former Bachelorette herself and an outspoken liberal, would join my cause. Bachelor Nation is known for being conservative, but I could think of several other liberal contestants who I was sure would join me. Another was Wells Adams, from JoJo's season. Surely he would speak up once I told him he had inspired my son's name.

Dane poked his head into the bedroom with a dozing Wells in his arms. "What are you doing?" he asked.

"Nothing. Just taking some notes on something I want to remember," I replied vaguely. I didn't want to tell Dane what I was really doing. He wouldn't understand how important this was. He would tell me I should be napping instead. It would be better for him not to know for now. He'd be proud of me once he saw how I'd single-handedly held ABC accountable for their actions.

*****

After spending over an hour hunched over my laptop working on the outline, my muscles felt tense and cramped. Despite the biting February air, I longed to stretch my legs and venture outside for a walk.

As much as I longed for a walk, there was a problem. My mind had become so scattered I was worried about wandering off course and getting lost. My sense of direction was spotty at the best of times and downright impaired at the moment. Although we'd lived in our neighborhood for nearly two years and I'd gone on thirty-minute walks every day during my pregnancy, I wasn't sure that would be enough to keep me from misremembering my path and heading in the wrong direction when I tried to go home.

To address the problem, I announced to Dane and my mom that I was going to start doing laps of our block. We lived on a street with a major throughway on one side and a T-junction on the other. Surely the traffic on the busy road would be enough to remind me not to cross, and running into the T would alert me that it was time to turn around.

"If you ever want to check on me, you can just look out the window and you'll be able to see me." I thought this would bring them comfort, but Dane looked alarmed.

"Are you saying you're worried about getting lost a few blocks away from our house? Even with your phone?"

I hadn't thought about Google Maps. But even then, I couldn't be sure I'd remember to use the tool in my pocket if I got frazzled about losing my way. "I mean, I think it's better to be on the safe side. I'll be like a mall walker, but on our street."

Dane didn't smile like I had expected him to.

"You should definitely bring this up when you start therapy on Monday," Dane said.

I laughed. "I doubt the therapists will care how bad I am with directions."

"But the fact that you're scared to leave our block . . . worries me."

"I'm not scared," I huffed. "I'm just being safe. I have a lot on my mind, and I don't want anything bad to happen to me."

"I don't want that either," Dane rushed to clarify. "But the fact that you think you might get lost in our own neighborhood seems like a red flag to me."

Poor Dane, I thought. Parenthood was turning him into such a worrier. He had never been like this before. He was always the calm one. He could think of a solution to any problem at the drop of a hat and never seemed to get flustered. There was no reason why my "mall walking" plan should upset him so much.

"Just promise me you'll ask about this on Monday," said Dane.

I shrugged. "If you want me to." But I had no intention of bringing up something so irrelevant in therapy.

*****

Having decided I could safely walk around the block, I decided to treat myself to a coffee at the shop at the end of our street after Wells's afternoon feeding. Settling in with my latte, I pulled out my phone to go through my emails. One particular email caught my eye. It was about a fundraiser for COVID-19 research sponsored by Everlane, one of my favorite clothing brands. All proceeds from purchases of a specific hat would go toward the project. My brain whirled into action. Fighting the coronavirus was such an important issue. I needed to do my part. I thought of my local group of friends and the GroupMe account we used for chatting and decided I needed to encourage all of them to buy the hat. I opened the app and started typing.

Jessica: Hi, friends. Slowly, but steadily, recovering postpartum lady checking in. As (almost all of) you know, my current phase of recovery involves a LOT of time just sitting, not doing much of anything. Some days, like today, I feel pretty good. Reasonably close to my Before Times Self (no, I don't mean the COVID Before Times, but rather the Jessica Before Times.) Other days, I feel like a mess. When I try to talk too much or even sit in a room where more than two people are speaking at once, my brain just freezes. It's a very strange experience, and I'm struggling to articulate it at this point. But thanks to Alyssa, I was immediately directed to a comprehensive, one-stop shop therapy program that I start on Monday. www.everlane.com/coronavirus.

Jessica: Oops, that Everlane link got sent too early, but that is going to become relevant later in this message.

Jessica: This, incidentally, is a good example of what my brain is doing at the moment.

Jessica: I knew I wanted to send you all a message so you would know how I'm doing. But I also knew I needed to prepare an outline first to refer to along the way, otherwise I'd sit here for hours, losing my train of thought constantly, and probably still couldn't send this message in one sitting.

It felt good to be able to write sentences the way they appeared in my head. My speech had started to become jumbled, and my sentences never seemed to come out quite as clear as I had intended. I took a sip of my latte and returned to my message, not wanting to keep my friends waiting on the rest of my update.

Jessica: I assume some of you have started reading this very long message by now, but have refrained from commenting yet, which I appreciate because I bet you already understand that this message is mentally hard for me to prepare, and you are supporting me right now by giving me time to focus and finish my message.

Jessica: You are right about that, and I appreciate your patience because focus is a very limited resource for me right now.

Jessica: One of the many reasons this message is so long is that I never know whether a day will be good or bad.

Jessica: Today is a pretty good day, so I wanted to update you now because I don't know when my next good day will be.

Jessica: I hope it's tomorrow, but who knows?

My phone rang, interrupting my chain of thought before I could make it back to the Everlane promotion. It was Alyssa, our friend who had referred me to the intensive outpatient therapy program.

"Hi, Jessica. I saw the messages you sent to the GroupMe chat." Her voice was calm and steady. "How are you feeling today?"

"I'm doing great," I announced. "Today was actually a good day. I've had a lot more energy than I was expecting to. I'm getting a lot done."

Alyssa hesitated. "I'm glad you're having a good day today. But I think you've shared enough in the chat for now and it would be good if you went home and did something relaxing."

I was confused. "But there's this hat. All the money raised goes to COVID research, and I want everyone to buy it."

"I think the hat can wait," Alyssa said gently. "Is there a relaxing activity you could do when you get home?"

This conversation was taking such a strange turn, I thought. Why didn't Alyssa want me to spread the word about the Everlane promotion? Why was she using her soothing social worker voice with me? I wasn't one of her clients. Sure, she told Dane about the therapy program, which was nice of her, but she didn't need to be monitoring my activities. Still, I didn't want to be rude. Alyssa was a good friend, and I was sure she meant well. Dane's new parent stress had probably just rubbed off on her when they spoke. Stress is contagious.

"I could read," I said, even though I had no intention of doing so. I needed to get back to work on my outline of the letter to ABC. I didn't want the letter going out much later than the episode's air date. ABC needed to know how seriously I took their assault. They needed to pay to make things right, or else I'd expose them for the abusers they were.

"I think reading sounds like a great idea," said Alyssa.

"Okay. If you think it's best, I'll go home and do that." I didn't want to add to Alyssa's stress. She had two kids of her own, plus her demanding social work job at the high school. Dane shouldn't have made her start worrying about me on top of everything.

I said goodbye to Alyssa and sent a final message to the GroupMe chat: *"Ok, that's it for now. I'll update you all again soon."* I was surprised no one had responded to my message yet. Usually, the GroupMe chat was very active. Maybe everyone was writing long messages of support and encouragement and they'd come through later in the night. I put my phone in my coat pocket and walked back down the block toward home.

CHAPTER 7

DIVERSITY

Lying in bed and staring at the ceiling, I flexed and pointed my toes to ease the restlessness in my legs. I was wide awake. I had just put Wells down for his nap and was trying to get some sleep myself, but it wasn't going well. Sleeping hadn't gone well ever since we got home from the hospital. I was strangely never tired.

Plus, there was so much to do. Pump parts to clean, burp cloths to wash, and baby supplies to research and buy online. And that was before I set aside any time for myself. I wanted to keep doing the hobbies I loved and maintain my relationships with my friends. I didn't want to stop reading every day or slow my responses to text messages. I especially didn't want to be forgotten professionally. I was terrified of coming back to work and finding that all my assignments had been transferred permanently to other lawyers, or that my clients had decided to look for an attorney without a new parent's time constraints. I was determined to remain on people's radars during my four-month maternity leave.

Getting to where I was professionally had been as challenging as it was improbable. At age thirty-three, I was elected to the partnership of Pattishall, McAuliffe, Newbury,

Hilliard & Geraldson LLP, a boutique law firm specializing in trademark, copyright, and advertising law. I was the youngest partner by nearly ten years. I had a string of litigation victories to my name and was steadily building up my book of business. I had been selected as a "Rising Star" by Illinois Super Lawyers for the past three years. My career was nothing like what I had expected growing up.

People like me weren't supposed to have careers like mine. I grew up in a town with no stoplights, surrounded by corn and soybean fields. My school had to join forces with another one twenty minutes away to field most of our sports teams, as neither school had enough students to fill up their rosters. There were no AP or International Baccalaureate classes. There was, however, an active chapter of the Future Farmers of America.

When I decided on the University of Missouri for college, I was the only student in my forty-three-person class to pick an out-of-state school. I did it for the journalism program. The University of Missouri, known affectionately as Mizzou, was famous for its journalism school. Many of the most respected writers in the country had trained there, and I wanted to be one of them.

Writing had always been a passion for me. It was the perfect activity for an only child. I loved how beautiful words could be, and how powerful when strung together in the right way. I loved compelling stories that sucked you in and stayed on your mind long after you finished reading them. I founded my high school's first newspaper and had an internship at a small city paper thirty minutes away, where I wrote stories about volunteers who built floats for the annual Christmas parade and the family who owned the beloved local fried chicken restaurant. My dream was to write for the *St. Louis*

Post-Dispatch. I knew I wanted to get out of my small town but moving somewhere like New York City or Los Angeles seemed much too overwhelming. St. Louis seemed manageable. I wanted my goals to be realistic.

When I arrived at Mizzou, I was surprised by my journalism professors' attitudes toward the profession. To their credit, they were honest about the direction the journalism world was moving. Newspapers across the country were closing and freelance writers and bloggers were taking their place. It was becoming harder and harder to be a classic newspaper journalist, which is what I had my heart set on. I wanted a desk in a bustling newsroom with a tip line and an editor and a giant printing press. Before long, it became clear to me that a career as a reporter might not be feasible. At least, it didn't seem likely.

I decided to switch paths. I had taken a class on media law and had been fascinated by the professor's stories about working as an attorney for a string of newspapers. She was constantly solving interesting and complex problems and spent her days reading, writing, and researching. It sounded like a great life. I switched my majors to political science and psychology and decided to go to law school.

I spent months attending LSAT prep classes and taking practice tests. My scores were good enough to get me into a midrange school but weren't anything special. With zero expectations of getting in, I applied to the University of Chicago, one of the top five law schools in the country. I thought it would be nice to be within driving distance of my parents, and Dane, who planned to move with me when I started law school, grew up in the suburbs.

My LSAT score was well below the twenty-fifth percentile at U of C, but I thought there was a tiny chance my 4.0 GPA, membership on the college mock trial team, and designation as a Phi Beta Kappa might warrant at least a moment of consideration. I was stunned when I got in.

It felt like a life designed for another person, not a girl from the middle of nowhere. My father was a self-employed real estate appraiser, and my mother was a telephone customer service representative. I had gone to a tiny high school and a public college. There was nothing remotely fancy about me. Yet, I was on my way to one of the most prestigious institutions in the country.

I spent my first trimester at U of C fighting extreme imposter syndrome. Although no one talked about LSAT scores, I felt like mine was a dirty little secret. I was self-conscious about my public school pedigree. Most of my classmates had gone to Ivy League schools or elite liberal arts colleges on the East Coast. Very few went to schools like Mizzou.

But as the year progressed, I began to grow more confident. Despite all the horror stories I had heard before enrolling, I loved law school. It wasn't the cutthroat, joyless environment pictured in pop culture. It was engaging and challenging. My classmates and professors were insightful and endlessly interesting. They had lived a multitude of lives. I had a former state representative in my class, along with an animal rights activist, collegiate athletes, teachers, and everything in-between. I got immense satisfaction from making sense of the cases we read, parsing the language, and drawing analogies. My brain was constantly buzzing with new ideas and connections.

I instantly fell into a close-knit group of friends. We created what we called The Ethnic Dining Alliance—TEDA for short—and went out for dinner every Friday night at a different ethnic restaurant. We took turns picking, and the rule was we couldn't repeat any specific ethnicity. We tried Costa Rican, Polish, and Ethiopian, crisscrossing our way around the city as the months rolled by. Before our winter formal one year, we ate dinner at a Romanian restaurant that sent a battered limousine to pick us up. We dubbed it Rom Prom.

After my first year in law school, I participated in the on-campus interviewing program. I secured a summer internship at Pattishall for the following year. At the end of the internship, I was offered a full-time position upon graduation. I gleefully accepted and had been with the firm ever since.

After years of hard work and good fortune, I was determined to keep my career thriving while I was out on maternity leave. I considered the options. I could take on some kind of pro bono assignment while I was out. Or I could write an article for one of the legal journals. But what I really wanted was to remain top-of-mind for my clients. I decided the best thing to do would be to increase my presence on LinkedIn. I would write thoughtful posts and substantive comments on other people's content. That way, all my clients would see I was remaining connected to the legal world, even as a new parent.

I got out of bed, grabbed my laptop, and settled myself on the couch. My parents were downstairs in the guest room, and Dane had gone out for a walk. The living room was calm and quiet. I logged into LinkedIn and got to work.

A quick scroll brought up a post from an employee of a fitness company I represent. A local business publication had named the company a start-up to watch. "Well deserved! I'm proud to be part of a team that's truly making a difference in people's health and lives," I wrote. I might as well remind any would-be client poachers that this company was already represented, and by an attorney who took the time to engage with their social media content, no less. It was important to mark my territory.

I continued scrolling and came across a post from one of my colleagues, who had been named to the Illinois Super Lawyers list. "After all these years, you're still the smartest lawyer I know," I wrote. It couldn't hurt to stay top-of-mind within the firm too. I wanted my fellow partners to remember I'd be back in a few months and ready to return to business.

Turning back to my feed, I saw a post from an attorney I'd met years ago at a networking event. She was inviting people to submit applications for an award for women lawyers being offered by one of the city's legal magazines. Jackpot, I thought. I could mention a slew of lawyers I knew and encourage them all to apply for the award. They would be flattered that I thought of them, and I could connect with a whole group of fellow attorneys at once. I combed through my mental Rolodex and tagged fifteen or twenty local lawyers, saying I thought any of them were more than qualified to win the award. I submitted the comment.

I realized I should do more. The women I'd named in my comment were mostly white. The number of minority lawyers I knew was embarrassingly small. But it was extra important for lawyers of color to be considered for awards like this. Their careers were already uphill battles spent fighting against discrimination and unfair assumptions. I should be doing something to help them.

I'd always had a complicated personal relationship with the idea of minority status. My mother was born and raised in Colombia, and all my family on her side still lived there.

I grew up speaking Spanish and visited Colombia every few years. I was objectively a Latina. But with pale skin, medium brown hair, and my father's German last name, no one ever guessed I was anything other than a garden-variety white woman. It made me feel like I wasn't "allowed" to be a Latina. I didn't join the Latin Students Association in college, and I had very few fellow Latin people in my social circle. I never knew which option to pick when asked for my ethnicity on forms.

The summer before I started law school, I was invited to apply for Sponsors for Educational Opportunity, an organization that aims to give minority students a leg up in the corporate world. They offered a program that paired soon-to-be law students with some of the most prestigious law firms in New York for paid summer internships, then offered a two-week boot camp to prepare participants for law school. The boot camp included simulated law school classes and exams. I knew law schools used the Socratic method, a teaching style where professors pick students at random to pepper with questions. I had read that being called on, especially on a day when you felt underprepared, shoved a dagger of fear into every first-year law student's heart. And the exams were an entirely foreign concept. Rather than the multiple choice and essay questions I'd been asked to complete in college, law school would introduce me to "issue spotters," hypothetical cases where I would be required to identify all the legal issues raised and then analyze how to solve them. I felt entirely unprepared for both the Socratic method and this new style of exam, and I longed for the opportunity to take part in SEO's crash course.

But I was hesitant to apply. What would the program think when they saw my last name or took in my face during the interview process? Would they think I was lying about meeting the program's qualifications? What would the other SEO scholars make of me? Would they think I didn't deserve to be there? It was true that neither my last name nor my face had ever led to me being the victim of discrimination, like other minority students. I wasn't sure whether I was entitled to the benefits SEO could provide. But, on the other hand, I was a proud, Spanish-speaking Colombian, and on paper I met all the criteria to apply for the program. With no lawyers in my immediate family or circle of friends, I was desperate for help preparing myself for the rigors of law school. I was torn.

In the end, I decided to apply. A whiff of guilt surrounded me whenever I worked on my application, but I decided the potential benefits SEO could offer outweighed my discomfort. Besides, I really was a Latina.

I was thrilled when I was accepted into the program, although I spent the entire summer grappling with a lingering sense that perhaps I had taken the spot of someone who deserved it more than me. Someone who got followed around in clothing stores or ignored when they raised their hand in class. Someone who would be paid less than their white counterparts and assumed to be inferior at work until proven otherwise. None of those things had ever happened to me.

I thought about my experience in SEO as I considered what else to say in my LinkedIn comments. Maybe this was an opportunity to atone for my possible sins.

"Feel free to nominate any other women lawyers you think are deserving, especially women of color!" I added a new comment beneath my initial one. But then I realized I needed a disclaimer. I didn't want people to think I considered a simple social media post sufficient in terms of doing my part to fight racism.

"I want to acknowledge that my post above isn't nearly enough. It's easy to post things on social media, but what we really need to do is hire and promote attorneys of color."

I considered this. I wasn't the hiring partner at my firm and didn't have much say in hiring or promotion decisions. But maybe I could get the word out to people who were. No, it was more than a maybe. Surely I could make a difference here. I had an impressive network filled with partners, general counsels, and other high-profile attorneys. To whom much is given, much is expected, I thought. The responsibility of getting attorneys of color the opportunities they deserved clearly fell on my shoulders.

I began adding more and more comments to the post about the women attorneys' award.

"People with hiring authority need to put their money where their mouths are. They say there's a pipeline problem and that's why they're not able to hire diverse talent, but the real problem is they're not willing to put in the effort to find minority candidates. They don't bother going to the HBCU job fairs and then they're surprised they've got an applicant pool filled with white dudes."

I chuckled to myself. I knew I was being a bit subversive, but I felt the situation warranted it. The legal industry's failure to recruit and retain attorneys of color was a serious problem, and I needed to use my power to address it. My brain kicked into overdrive, and I could feel the flood of ideas crashing in and battling each other for prominence. I tried to focus on one thing at a time, but I was suddenly inundated with thoughts, each seeming more crucial than the last. I began frantically typing, trying to capture each idea before it vanished.

"Sidenote: Moaning about your lack of diverse employees, while refusing to bother looking for diverse talent where it already is, is like talking about 'thoughts and prayers' during a national disaster. It eases your guilty conscience, but it doesn't accomplish anything."

"Sidenote to the sidenote (I know! So many sidenotes!): Do you know who the people are who are always moaning about their lack of diverse employees, but not doing anything to solve the problem? White dudes. And do you know why? Because, deep down, they want their companies to be filled with other white dudes just like them, so they can feel comfortable and cozy and play ping-pong in the middle of the day and make sexist jokes without any repercussions and bump their chests during team meetings."

Now I was on a roll. I felt bold and brave. I had never seen anyone use LinkedIn to call out the systemic discrimination issues plaguing the legal profession. And doing it in such an unexpected, provocative tone would surely bring even more attention to what I was saying. I couldn't recall ever seeing a mention of a "white dude" on LinkedIn.

"Sidenote to the sidenote to the sidenote (And here you thought there couldn't be any more sidenotes! But then there were! Eeeek!): Do you know the one thing that makes the white dudes mad about not having any diverse employees at their company? The fact that they don't get to win any diversity awards. When they respond to requests for proposals that ask them about diversity in their workforce, they don't have anything good to say. They don't get any diversity brownie points. And white dudes want ALL the brownie points. They don't want anyone else to get a single brownie point (especially not brown people, ha!). The only reason white dudes might actually care about recruiting diverse talent is so they can brag about how open-minded and forward-thinking they are in their marketing materials. And so they can end up on all the top twenty lists. Twenty Best Places to Work, Twenty Most Inclusive Workplaces, all of that. White dudes want all the brownie points and they also want to win all of the awards. They think they deserve them. They think—"

"Jessica?" Dane's voice brought my frantically typing fingers to a halt. "What are you doing?" He was frowning.

I considered his question. Something told me I shouldn't tell him what I was doing. Just like I didn't think he'd understand why I needed to write the letter to ABC, I didn't think he'd understand why I needed to make sure diverse attorneys were given fair chances to be hired and promoted. He would probably tell me I didn't need to worry about this right now, less than a week after I had given birth. It would be too hard to explain.

"I'm just answering an email." I hated lying to Dane, but I had to do it.

"Okay. You've been on your computer a lot lately. Maybe you should take a break."

"You're right." I quickly closed my laptop before Dane could see what I was doing. I would come back to this later. There was so much left to say.

CHAPTER 8

PROVING MYSELF

Tilting my head back into the spray of the shower, the deluge of thoughts running through my mind felt almost like a physical weight. I had tried listening to my audiobook on the waterproof Bluetooth speaker, but my thoughts were racing too much to concentrate. I finally decided to just give in to the internal chaos and let my mind run free, hoping it would burn off enough energy to settle.

I thought about what we were having for dinner that night. My friend Bren had organized a meal train, and delicious spreads from all our favorite local restaurants had been showing up nightly since we'd gotten home. This led me to think about how we would find time to cook dinner once we'd both gone back to work. Would one of us cook while the other picked Wells up from day care? Would we have time to eat as a family? Would it be possible to feed Wells and eat at the same time? Thinking about balancing work and life led me to thoughts about my job. Would I be able to bill enough hours as a new mom? Or would I let down my entire sex by fulfilling the stereotype of the woman who has a baby and checks out from work?

On and on my thoughts spiraled, one feeding into the next without a break in between. It was exhausting. I craved a moment of mental stillness. I tried to focus on the sensation of warm, humid air entering my nostrils, but immediately got sidetracked by thoughts about yoga classes. When would I be able to return? Would I still have time for yoga? I used to exercise first thing in the morning. But now I'd need to tend to Wells as soon as he woke up every day. Where would working out fit into my new schedule?

I stepped out of the steam and wrapped my hair in a towel. I turned on the shower radio, which started playing our local NPR station. Maybe a few minutes of listening to the news would be grounding. The station was broadcasting an interview with a local doctor, who was discussing the newly available coronavirus vaccine. My ears seized on her words. This was exactly what my parents needed to hear. I was certain their conservative views would make them resistant to the vaccine. This interview was crucial. It could be the thing that convinced them about the seriousness of the pandemic and the importance of getting vaccinated. It could save their lives.

I threw on my bathrobe, barely pausing long enough to fasten the tie around my waist, and snatched the radio out of the shower, dribbling water onto the tile floor. I raced down the hallway on my damp feet and slammed the radio onto the kitchen table, where my parents and Dane were eating breakfast.

"This is important information!" I announced, slightly out of breath. It would have taken too much effort to explain what the topic of the broadcast was, so I decided to let the interview speak for itself.

My parents looked up from their plates at me, startled. My mother opened her mouth, presumably to ask me what was going on, but I pointed at the radio emphatically.

"Listen!" I said desperately.

She closed her mouth but continued eying me with concern. I didn't care. All that mattered was that my parents heard this doctor explain why the vaccine was safe and how important it was to get it.

The doctor wrapped up her overview and invited listeners to call in with questions. My eyes darted to my parents.

"Do you have any questions? Should we call?" I asked eagerly, grabbing a pen and a pad of Post-it notes to write down the phone number.

"I don't think we have any questions," my mother said carefully.

I cocked my head at her. "Really? What about your fibromyalgia? Don't you want to ask whether the vaccine could have any effect on that? Or your arthritis? Now's the time to ask. This doctor is giving away her time and advice for free," I enthused.

"I don't think we need to call in right now," my father chimed in.

I felt desperate. Surely there was something this doctor could say that would convince my parents to get the vaccine that could save their lives.

The segment ended, and I switched the radio off. I began pacing the kitchen with my hands clasped behind my back like a professor. "You need to get the vaccine as soon as you can. It's important to me that you believe the coronavirus is real and not a hoax and that you take it seriously." My thoughts began ramping up, and I became acutely aware of my heart starting to race in my chest. This was about more than just the pandemic. This was my opportunity to convince my parents to reevaluate the news sources they consumed and stop listening to conservative propaganda.

I grew up in a Fox News household. When I had the day off school as a kid, I'd ride around in my dad's truck with him as he conducted real estate appraisals. Rush Limbaugh prattled on in the background as my dad gathered his tape measure and camera and searched the MLS books for properties to compare to his target.

My father welcomed the opportunity to impart his political views. Every morning when he waited for the school bus with me, he'd tell me a story. The stories were all set in the fictional town of Maxville, Ohio, and featured best friends Jessica Jackrabbit, Sammy Snake, and Max Mouse. Jessica Jackrabbit's life mirrored my own. When I had a mean teacher in second grade, so did Jessica Jackrabbit. When I started playing second base on the softball team, so did she. One of the recurring minor characters in Jessica Jackrabbit's universe was Bud Smalley, union leader of the Amalgamated Brotherhood of Widgetworkers International. Bud had a high-pitched, nasal voice and a chronic stutter, and was forever botching everything he tried to accomplish. My father had a very specific opinion about unions, one he wanted to pass along to me.

So when the pandemic hit, I was terrified that my parents' conservative news sources would convince them that it was overblown or, worse, a plot by liberal elites to take over the world. I had read about a rumor circulating on Facebook that the nasal swabs used in COVID-19 tests were ways for Bill Gates to secretly implant microchips in peoples' brains so he could track them. To me, such a story seemed laughable, but it wasn't at all funny how many people believed everything they read on social media.

    I continued pacing the kitchen, preparing myself to give my very best argument in favor of the vaccination. I felt like I was making a final, impassioned plea at an oral hearing. My years of legal training were all leading up to this moment.

    "I know you probably don't believe COVID is real, but it is. Hundreds of thousands of people have already died from it, and Trump made it worse by downplaying everything. He made it seem like it wasn't a big deal and it was no worse than catching the flu, but it's completely different. Mom, with your history of asthma and your pacemaker, and all your health issues, you could end up on a ventilator. This is very, very serious."

    My mother opened her mouth to respond, but I held out my hand to silence her.

    "Don't interrupt me," I demanded. "I need to say this."

    My mother pursed her lips and shot my father a look, but said nothing.

    "I know the news sources you listen to are probably telling you the pandemic isn't real, but they're wrong. There's no other way to say it. You need to believe in science. This is a time when you need to be listening to the experts, not politicians and commentators who are just trying to fire people up. COVID being real is a fact, and you need to believe in facts. We live in this post-truth world where there are conspiracy theories and hackers and impersonations and deep fakes, but COVID is real and you have to believe that. You just have to." My words came racing out in desperation. I hadn't let my parents get a word in edgewise, but I felt confident I had proven my case. Surely they would take my words to heart and get the vaccine as soon as they were eligible.

But forcing my racing thoughts into a coherent argument had taken a toll on me. My brain was swirling so quickly I could barely see straight. I was starting to get confused. Had I just been giving a lecture in my kitchen? Why? Why were my parents staring at me in silence? Why was Dane scrubbing the same pot over and over and refusing to look at me? It was all too much.

"I'm going to go rest," I announced abruptly. And without waiting for anyone to respond, I rushed down the hallway to our bedroom, closing the door behind me.

Alone in the quiet room, I crawled onto our bed and pulled a pillow into my lap, hugging it for comfort. A blanket of fear started settling over me. Something was wrong. Scenes from the past few days flashed through my mind. The fear in Dane's eyes when I tried to initiate the improv scene about the missing towel. Throwing myself to the ground to hide from the DCFS agents I feared were lurking outside. Alyssa telling me in her best social worker voice that I needed to stop telling our friends about the Everlane promotion and go home to relax. And, worst of all, Dane saying he thought I needed to join an intensive therapy program instead of just seeing a weekly counselor as I had in the past.

What was happening to me? Was I losing my mind? Would I be forced into a psychiatric hospital? My stomach roiled at the thought. Being locked away in some horrible asylum was an absolute nightmare scenario. But what if it came to that? What if the therapists in the intensive outpatient program thought I was a lost cause? What if I needed some sort of medical intervention? Was electroshock therapy still a thing? Would insurance cover it? If not, how much would it cost?

My mind began spinning faster and faster. It was becoming clear to me that this might be an emergency and I needed to be prepared. I could end up locked away in a psychiatric ward needing expensive treatment with no way to pay for it. I had to make sure that didn't happen. My mind jumped to my and Dane's emergency fund.

When we were first married, we had gone to see a financial planner. His biggest piece of advice was to create a fund with six months' worth of living expenses in it in case of an unexpected job loss or medical issue. We obediently followed his advice. I realized I needed to make sure Dane could access the money in the account if I was locked away. The bank might require permission from both of us to empty the account.

I grabbed a pen and the notebook I left on my nightstand for jotting down to-do items. I began writing feverishly.

My name is Jessica Andrea Ekhoff.

My birthday is October 22, 1986.

My social security number is 349-94-9232.

I graduated from Brimfield High School in 2005, the University of Missouri in 2009, and the University of Chicago Law School in 2012.

I am married to Dane Michael Canada. We got married on April 18, 2012, in Columbia, Missouri. Our son is Wells Canada-Ekhoff, born February 9, 2021.

My mother is Nohora Ekhoff. She was born in Bogotá, Colombia. Her mother was Alicia Botero Tellez. My father is John Marshall Ekhoff. His parents are Ray and Ruth Ekhoff.

I live at 237 Potomac Avenue, Chicago, Illinois 60622. We bought our condo in April 2019.

I am an attorney at Pattishall McAuliffe. My attorney identifiation number is 6932939.

You can prove I am who I say I am by comparing my penmanship to examples of things I have written around the house (note to Dane: gather several examples: grocery lists, birthday cards, etc.).

I have now proven my identity.

I, Jessica Andrea Ekhoff, Esq. give Dane Michael Canada consent to remove all funds from Ally bank account number 782332120 to pay for the treatment needed for this mental health emergency.

By the time I finished, my hands were shaking so badly I could barely sign and date my statement. My palms were sweaty, and my robe stuck to my skin. I heard the beginnings of a cry from the nursery next door. Wells went from asleep to screaming for food in no time flat, and I knew he would begin to melt down if I didn't feed him soon. I disentangled my trembling legs from the sheets and stumbled to the door.

CHAPTER 9

THE INTERVIEW

I could see Dane's impatient face in the mirror as I began applying eyeliner.

"Are you almost ready?" he asked, checking his watch. It was Saturday morning, and we were supposed to have left for my intake interview with the intensive outpatient therapy program five minutes ago.

"Stop rushing me," I grumbled. "I know you don't think so, but it's important for me to look my best. They need to see that I'm sane and put together and not some crazy person who needs to be locked away. What I look like will be part of their assessment; I just know it will be."

Dane sighed. "You just gave birth. No one is going to judge you based on your appearance. They'll probably be impressed you showered and managed to wear matching shoes."

I put down my eyeliner pen. "Appearances always matter. People don't like to admit that, but they do. It's just like at work. Real lawyers wear blazers. If you don't wear a blazer, no one takes you seriously. And here, good moms look put together. They have enough organization and time management skills to take care of their babies and still put on nice outfits and some makeup. Someone who can make themself look presentable isn't crazy and doesn't need to be put in a psychiatric hospital. They need to see that I can do that. I'm not going to risk getting locked up because of what I look like at this interview." I turned my attention back to the mirror and began applying mascara to my lashes.

I was proud of the outfit I had carefully assembled for my interview. I was wearing black leggings and a black and white sweater with a V-neck and a flattering drape that minimized the roundness of my postpartum stomach. I had put on stud earrings and a delicate chain necklace. My fingers were still too swollen to wear my wedding ring, so I placed a small gold band I'd received from my mother on my ring finger instead. The outfit made me look competent and self-assured, but not like I was trying too hard. A different type of crazy person might dress up too much for an intake interview with a therapy program.

"I'm ready," I announced, grabbing my coat and bag from the hallway closet.

My dad and Dane were coming with me to the interview while my mom stayed home with Wells. We climbed into my dad's truck with Dane in the front and me in the back seat. I needed to concentrate. I had a small notebook with me, and I planned to outline what I'd say to the intake coordinator. A good mom would prepare for an important interview like this, and I was a good mom.

I repeated in my head the phrase Dane and I had come up with to describe what was happening to me. We had decided it was important not to use the word "psychosis." Psychotic people ended up in psych wards, and I refused to let that happen to me. Instead, I planned to describe my situation as a "postpartum mental health episode." This sounded serious enough that they would surely let me into the therapy program, but not so serious that they would force me into inpatient treatment.

Heading toward the building, I tucked my hand into the crook of Dane's elbow. My mind was so scattered that I couldn't focus on signs long enough to read them. I didn't want the receptionist to see me standing for too long in front of a sign trying to comprehend it. She might report my behavior to the interviewer. Instead, I allowed Dane to steer me to the front desk where I received a clipboard with forms to complete.

Settling into a chair in the corner of the waiting room, farthest away from the TV, I prepared myself to fill out the forms. It was critical that I fill them out perfectly. Any mistake I made could be used against me.

I lined up my water bottle and a granola bar, my notebook for outlining before I wrote anything on the forms, my headphones to block out the distracting sounds of the waiting room, and my best pen. It bore the name of an expensive members-only social club downtown where the board of directors of my law school alumni association met for our monthly meetings. Crazy people didn't have pens from fancy social clubs, I reasoned. If anyone came to check on me while I was filling out my forms, I hoped they would see the name on my pen and report it to the interviewer. It would be a point in my favor.

I decided to fill my half-empty water bottle before beginning so I wouldn't have to stop midway through completing the forms and break my concentration. When I got to the water fountain, however, I saw it was out of order. I was furious. How dare this facility fail to fix its water fountain and deprive the scared, stressed people in their waiting room of one of the most basic, life-sustaining resources?

I rushed back to where Dane and my father were sitting. "Can you find a gas station or something and buy a few twenty-four-packs of bottled water?" I asked them.

My father frowned. "Why?"

"The water fountain is broken, and these people deserve to have water," I said, gesturing around the waiting room. "Water is a basic human right. It's not supposed to be just for people who can afford to buy it. What if these people are poor? What if they can't buy their own bottled water? It's not fair that they don't get to have water when they're stuck in this waiting room and the water fountain is broken."

I looked around the room. A middle-aged Hispanic woman and two teenagers in shabby winter coats huddled in one corner. A man with mussed hair sat across from them, rubbing his fingertips together and muttering to himself. Two young women sat close together, staring dully at their phones. These people deserved water every bit as much as I did.

"I know it's not our responsibility," I continued. "This place needs to get its act together and fix its water fountain, but in the meantime, we're in a position to do something good here. These people should have access to clean drinking water, and we can give that to them. When you're in a position to do some good in the world, you should take it."

My father shot Dane an exasperated look. "I'll go see what I can find," he said, rising from his seat and pulling his wool hat back onto his head.

"Thank you," I said. "It's the right thing to do." I took a small sip from my bottle, careful to conserve the resource until my father returned, and started the forms.

The first few questions were simple: name, address, phone number, birthday. Then things got more complicated. The form asked what my living status was. The options were "alone," "with significant other/spouse," "with children/family members," and "other." I was confused. Spouses were family members. Was I supposed to check both boxes? What if I was only allowed to check one box? Was this a trick? Why couldn't this place do a better job of wording its forms so people who are already stressed didn't have to be confused on top of everything? I decided to err on the side of caution. I checked "other," then wrote in the margin of the form, "I live with my husband and son. Not clear whether 'family members' is meant to exclude spouses, since the preceding choice is 'significant other/spouse.' For the avoidance of doubt, I selected 'other' and listed the people who live with me." I felt proud of myself. This form was clearly trying to trick me, but I hadn't let it. I had been clear and thorough. Surely, I wouldn't lose any points for that.

I moved on to the emergency contact section and hit another stumbling block. The form asked for Dane's work phone number. Dane didn't have a direct phone line at his job. But if I left the answer box blank, would the interviewer assume Dane was unemployed? Would that be a bad thing? What if they decided to take Wells away because they thought we weren't in a financial position to support him? I wrote "n/a" with an asterisk, then noted that Dane was employed but didn't have a work phone number. Then I returned to an earlier section that asked about my own employment and added "equity partner" to "IP attorney." I needed to make it clear that we had money. We were financially responsible and entirely capable of taking care of Wells. I didn't want to leave any wiggle room for contrary assumptions.

The stress of not letting the forms get the best of me was beginning to weigh on me. I felt fatigued. The TV droned from the wall and interrupted my thoughts, even with my headphones on. The Hispanic mother's conversation with her two children drifted over from the corner. I couldn't concentrate. I went to the front desk and asked if there was a quiet place I could go to finish my forms. The receptionist directed me to a small prayer room next to the waiting room. I balked. I wasn't a religious person. What did it mean if I filled out my forms in the prayer room?

I hadn't always been this way. I'd grown up going to the Lutheran church in my small town. I went to Vacation Bible School during the summers and completed confirmation classes in junior high. My confirmation ceremony was one of the few events of mine that my grandparents made time to attend. They sat in the front row and sang the hymns louder than anyone. During the call and response, my grandfather's "Amen" rung out above everyone else's.

In high school, I accompanied a friend to "Wesley Weekend," a two-day lock-in sponsored by her church. Sincere-eyed teenagers made posters about their favorite biblical values and sat in a circle after dinner sharing their deepest insecurities over popcorn and lukewarm Sprite. The boy I'd had a crush on for years was at the lock-in, and I felt myself growing even more attracted to him as I listened to him explain the meaning behind his poster. It was important for me to be with a godly person.

In college, I became curious about denominations outside of the Lutheranism I had always known. I had been spending more and more time thinking about the church I grew up in, and especially the pastor I used to follow blindly, and wondering whether all of it was still a good fit. Pastor Jackson's favorite catchphrase had been, "God made Adam and Eve, not Adam and Steve." Finally outside the conservative homogeneity of my hometown, I had made my first gay friend and started to wonder whether perhaps my pastor had been wrong. Didn't Lance deserve to love the person he felt attracted to, even if that was another man? Surely a loving God wouldn't reject him for simply following his heart. If God created man in His own image, then didn't it follow that being gay must be one of many natural states of being, just like being brunette or having freckles? And if Lutheranism was wrong about same-sex relationships, then couldn't it be wrong about other things too?

To try to answer these questions, I had taken myself on a "Tour of Denominations." Each week I went to a new church, searching for something that clicked. I went to churches with names familiar from my childhood, like Methodist and Episcopalian, but also spent time with the Christian Scientists and Pentecostals. I'd even seen someone speak in tongues. But the longer I searched, the less sure I was I'd ever find a church that felt right. Each church was restrictive in its own way, and I couldn't help but notice not a single one was led by a woman.

This was particularly problematic to me. College had taught me that being a feminist wasn't reserved for "fat, ugly" women, as my hometown had led me to believe. In fact, I had become comfortable identifying myself using what I had once heard referred to mockingly as "the other F word." I felt uneasy participating in a religion guided by a book that relegated women to the roles of cook, child-bearer, and fabric weaver.

I was already primed to leave organized religion behind when I met Dane. It was the summer of 2007 at the University of Missouri. We had both been selected as Summer Welcome Leaders, two of the thirty-six college students who lived on campus all summer and gave tours, led question and answer sessions, and performed skits for the incoming freshmen and their families. It was an intense job with long hours, but immensely fun. The thirty six of us bonded quickly and soon felt like we'd known each other much longer than a few months.

Although I had a serious boyfriend at the time, Dane caught my eye early on. He had bright blue eyes, an adorable gap between his two front teeth, and an air of calm confidence. I found him intriguing. As the summer progressed, we started gravitating toward each other more and more. We sat together while stuffing folders with information packets at night and took the Summer Welcome golf carts out for joyrides around campus. Over Fourth of July weekend, all thirty six of us headed to the Chicago suburbs to stay with Dane's parents and explore the city. I shared Dane's childhood bedroom with him, although the two of us hadn't so much as kissed yet. At one point, Dane's mother cornered me in the kitchen and asked me pointedly, "So how long have you been dating my son?" I blushed deeply and denied any romantic entanglement, but Dane's mom had been looking into our future. We had our first kiss at the Navy Pier fireworks, and I broke up with my boyfriend when I returned from the trip.

On paper, it didn't make sense for Dane and I to be together. I was a Republican (although beginning to question that particular affiliation), and he was a Democrat. I grew up in a nine-hundred-person farm town, and he grew up in an affluent Chicago suburb. I was an extrovert, and he was an introvert. But most notably, I was a Christian, and he was an atheist. This was a major point of concern for me, so much so that I briefly got back together with my churchgoing ex-boyfriend, who seemed to make more sense as a match. But I was quickly drawn back to Dane. He was the kindest, least judgmental, most generous person I had ever met. He was the best person I knew, yet he didn't believe in God. It seemed irreconcilable. I had thought all the best people were fellow believers. It had never occurred to me that someone so good could be so wholly unconnected from Christianity. It made me wonder—was religion not a prerequisite to being a good person after all? Could I walk away from the male-dominated church world without damaging my soul? Did I need to bow my head every Sunday to be a good person, or could I achieve goodness in another way?

I began to identify less and less as a Christian, until one day a new label presented itself to me: agnostic. I still believed in God, but not the rest of it. No animals marching two-by-two into an enormous arc, no one living inside the belly of a whale. And, most importantly, no women created from the ribs of men for the purpose of serving them.

I hadn't attended church in years, and spending time in a space designated as a prayer room made me uncomfortable. But I couldn't concentrate on the forms in the noisy waiting room, so I gathered my belongings and begrudgingly made my way into the quiet space.

I settled into a chair by a wall lined with what appeared to be Sunday school drawings. They featured crosses surrounded by lists of blessings, and I paused to think about what I felt thankful for. A healthy baby boy who, despite the nurse's dire warnings, had not been afflicted by jaundice. A husband who was my equal partner and was already proving himself to be a warmhearted and loving father. Parents who loved me and were proud of me. A standing Wednesday night phone date with my best friend, Leigh Anne, who had been a fellow Summer Welcome Leader with Dane and me. An income that allowed me to take a vacation every year and live in a four-bedroom condo in one of Chicago's trendiest neighborhoods. On the whole, I was incredibly lucky, but it was hard to feel like it with the sheaf of intake forms in my hand, barely a week after having Wells.

I turned my attention back to the second page of the forms. The questions were becoming more and more confusing, and I increasingly had the sense they were designed to trick me into admitting something that would result in Wells being taken away. The weight of staying vigilant against any mistakes settled uncomfortably in my chest. I couldn't live with myself if I was the reason our baby got swept up into the foster care system.

The question asking whether I drank alcohol made me pause. Did it mean ever? Or today? Or more than a glass here and there with dinner? I panicked. This question was clearly designed to make me look like a drunkard incapable of taking care of a newborn. But I had to answer honestly. Last night, after Wells went to bed, I'd had a glass of Cabernet Sauvignon while I struggled to focus on one of my baby books. There was no way to avoid confessing. So I checked the "yes" box, but then added a second asterisk and a disclaimer: "Only after I finished nursing my son and expected him to sleep for approximately three hours. I know it is unsafe to breastfeed less than two hours after drinking alcohol. Before I drank the glass of wine, I confirmed we had bottles and formula in case he woke up earlier than expected. Additionally, my husband and both of my parents were home with me while I drank the glass of wine." There. That should prove that not only was I familiar with the rules around drinking while breastfeeding but also that I made sure Wells could be fed safely even if I had a bit of wine. The disclaimer squeezed in and out of the available blank space on the page, curving between questions. The form looked cramped, but I decided it was more important I be thorough with my answers.

Next, the form asked whether I had access to any weapons. Yet another trick question. Surely no authority would want a baby living in a home with guns. But again, I couldn't lie about the fact that I could walk into a gun shop and buy a gun tomorrow if I felt like it. This question was apparently trying to assess not only the safety of my home for Wells but also my honesty. Rather than answer the question by checking one of the boxes, I drew three asterisks and wrote, "Technically yes, in the sense I could likely obtain a weapon if I wanted one, just like everyone else in this country (unfortunately). But I don't want a weapon. Dane and I are both very opposed to having weapons in our home, especially now that we have a baby." My answer snaked sideways up the page and continued across the top. Along with my other disclaimers, the form was barely legible. But at least I hadn't left anything out. I had been forthcoming, thoughtful, and comprehensive, just as a good mother should be. I was proud of myself for protecting Wells from being snatched away from us by DCFS. Surely we could give him a better home than some do-gooder stranger.

I slowly made my way through the rest of the questions, stopping periodically for sips of water and bites of my granola bar. I had been in the prayer room for over two hours. When I finished, I took pictures of each page of the forms using a scanner app and carefully labeled each image. It was critical to keep records at a time like this. If someone tried to use the forms against me, I wanted to be able to prove exactly what I had said. I couldn't risk someone tampering with my answers.

I handed my forms to the receptionist and took a seat next to Dane in the waiting room. My father had returned, but there was no bottled water in sight.

"Did you buy the water?" I asked my father anxiously. Had these poor people been sitting in the waiting room while I completed my forms without anything to drink? Maybe I should have gone to buy the water myself. It was so hard to trust people. They just weren't reliable. It was no wonder I preferred to do things myself rather than delegate.

My father looked irritated. "It's not our job to give people water. And besides, there's another water fountain down the hall, and it works just fine."

I got up and hurried down the hall to see for myself. He was right. I felt a rush of relief. I hadn't let everyone down after all.

I walked back to my seat but couldn't sit still. I was nervous about my interview. I felt relatively certain I hadn't said anything in the forms that could be used to prove I was an unfit mother, but what if I misspoke during the interview? I had filled out the forms painstakingly slowly to avoid any mistakes, but I wouldn't be able to do that during the interview. If I spoke too slowly, it would seem suspicious. The interviewer might think I was choosing my words carefully because I was lying.

I got up and went to the bathroom. I gazed at myself in the large mirror above the row of sinks. I smoothed my hair and moved my necklace clasp to the back of my neck. Then I started practicing. "I am having a postpartum mental health episode," I said, watching my lips move. Too slow. It sounded like a script. "I am having a postpartum mental health episode," I repeated, a bit faster this time. Better. It sounded more natural at that speed. "I think I could really benefit from the intensive therapy program," I said to myself, gazing directly into the mirror. It would be important to maintain eye contact during the interview. Eye contact makes people trust you.

I decided to rehearse what I would say if the interviewer asked me what symptoms I was experiencing. I needed to toe the line between making my symptoms sound serious enough to let me into the program, but not so serious that I'd be labeled as crazy. "I've been having a lot of problems since Wells was born," I said to my reflection. I kept my voice as steady as I could. "My brain won't slow down, and my thoughts are always racing. I haven't been able to concentrate. And one night I yelled a lot at my husband. I never yell at him. He thinks it would be good for me to do this therapy program, and I trust him."

There was a knock on the bathroom door. "Jessica?" Dane's voice called out. "Are you okay in there? The nurse just called your name."

"I'm just practicing for my interview," I said. "I'll be out in a minute."

I looked back at my reflection. "Postpartum mental health episode," I said. I took a deep breath in through my nose and out through my mouth. "I am having a postpartum mental health episode," I said one last time, before leaving the bathroom and following the nurse down the hall.

My father, Dane, and I crowded around a small table in the interview room across from a woman with black hair and thick-framed glasses.

"Why don't you tell me a bit about what brought you in today?" she said to me.

I repeated the lines I'd been practicing in the bathroom.

"How has your sleep been? I know it can be hard to prioritize sleep as a new mom."

"Fine. I'm not sleeping much, but I don't feel tired. Maybe it's the breastfeeding."

The woman frowned and jotted something down on her clipboard. "What about your mood? Have you been feeling sad? Crying a lot?"

I shook my head. "Not at all."

Despite the racing thoughts and the intermittent uneasy feeling that something might be wrong, I had been in an excellent mood all week. I felt motivated and accomplished. I was proud of myself for preparing the letter to ABC and for promoting attorneys of color on LinkedIn. And I loved being a mom.

The interviewer raised an eyebrow. "No mood swings at all? They're very common in the early postpartum period."

I shook my head. "No. I'm feeling great. I just think I could be doing even better if I was in this program." I smiled at Dane. I knew it would make him feel better to have me in therapy, and if that was what he wanted, I was willing to do it.

I saw the interviewer consulting a few papers and realized she had my intake forms. She took her time reviewing them, then told me they had space available in the intensive therapy program, and I could start on Monday.

I felt happy for Dane. Hopefully, this would help with his stress and make it easier for him to enjoy early parenthood, like I was.

CHAPTER 10

FIGHTING FOR THE LITTLE GUY

We realized the buzzer to our front gate had stopped working. This was a problem because our friends Zach and Kathleen had signed up for a meal train delivery that night, and we wouldn't be able to hear the delivery person when they arrived.

I decided to call the delivery company, DoorDash, to give them my cell phone number for the driver to call instead of using the buzzer. Dane and my mother had laid Wells out on the play mat in the living room, so I went to our bedroom where I could concentrate on the call. Listening to more than one person speak at once made my brain freeze up. I could almost feel my mind running after one voice, then screeching to a halt, abruptly switching directions, and chasing after the second voice instead. It was disorienting and frustrating.

I sat down on the bed and dialed DoorDash's customer service number. An automated message informed me all agents were assisting other customers. I waited. The hold music grated on my nerves and a wave of annoyance washed over me. Why was this taking so long? Why didn't DoorDash hire enough customer service representatives? I remained on hold, my irritation steadily ticking upward. It was over five minutes before my call was answered. I explained to the representative that our buzzer was broken and I wanted to leave my phone number for the delivery driver to call when they arrived. The agent apologized but said his computer system didn't give him a way to send messages to drivers who had already been dispatched.

I exploded.

"That's absurd!" I said. Then I quickly amended myself. "I'm not mad at you," I assured the representative. "This isn't your fault. DoorDash has given you this shitty software to work with that doesn't even let you do your job. They're setting you up to fail." I was getting heated. I could feel my heartbeat rising into my temples and my palms starting to sweat. "And you know what the worst part is? I bet they pay you the bare fucking minimum. They've probably hired some fancy lawyer to find a loophole to say you're an independent contractor and not an employee so they can get away with paying you less and not giving you any benefits." I was fuming. "I bet you're just trying to support your family and keep a roof over your head, you're getting paid basically nothing, and this fucking tech giant company can't even be bothered to give you functioning software so you can do your job." I realized I was yelling.

I quickly got up from the bed and went into the bathroom, closing the door behind me. I didn't want Dane or my mom to hear me yelling. They'd misunderstand and think something was wrong with me. They wouldn't have the context to know I was yelling for a good cause.

"I'm sure they've got all kinds of rounds of funding, and they're drowning in money they don't even know what to do with, and they won't even spend enough of it to design a software platform that works. And they're a tech company! This is their sole fucking purpose for existing! They can't even get the one thing they're supposed to do right, and they've still got all these investors begging to throw wads of money at their feet. It makes me sick!"

I paused.

"Are you recording me?" I demanded. It suddenly occurred to me that this recording could be used against me. What if it ended up being played on the news and I came off sounding unhinged? But I quickly dismissed the notion. This cause was important. This poor customer service representative was being taken advantage of by a soulless company that needed to be forced to change its ways. An idea was beginning to take shape in my mind.

"You know what? Fuck it. I hope you are recording me," I said, not giving the representative a chance to speak. "I've got a lot to say." I began pacing around the bathroom as I ranted, unable to stand still. "DoorDash has made the wrong person mad. I have time, I have resources, and I know all the right people. I'm going to do something about this. I've got four months of maternity leave ahead of me. All I do all day is sit in a chair and feed a baby, which requires zero thought. I've got this big lawyer brain, and it has nothing to do. It wants a project, and this is going to be it. I'm going to make DoorDash sorry they ever took advantage of you." I caught a glimpse of myself in the bathroom mirror and saw my cheeks had become a mottled red and my pupils were dilated.

But I couldn't stop.

"You know, a lot of people would probably just let this go and not do anything about it, but I'm not one of those people. I'm not a shitty rich person; I'm a good rich person. I'm just someone who ended up with a lot of money because of the job I do, but I'm not some asshole. I care about people. And I'm going to make DoorDash sorry for what it's doing to you."

"Jessica?" Dane's alarmed voice came from the other side of the bathroom door. He tried to open it, but I had locked it behind me so no one could come in and interrupt my monologue. What I was saying was important, and I wanted to make sure DoorDash heard every word when they listened to the recording of the call later. I wanted them to know I was coming for them.

"Jessica, stop yelling and unlock the door," Dane said. His voice sounded shaky.

"No! I'm not yelling at the customer service guy. I'm on his side! DoorDash is treating him horribly, and I'm going to do something about it!"

"You need to hang up. Hang up the phone and open the door," Dane pleaded.

I hesitated. Dane had been under so much stress lately. I got the sense he was still upset about me yelling at him a few days ago, and he was probably still mad at himself for burning Wells's pacifiers and putting us all in danger. He was obviously struggling. I didn't want to add to his burden.

"Let me just say one last thing," I said to the representative. "I'm going to fix this for you. I'm going to make it right. I promise. I'm going to use my money and my connections and my time to do something good in the world. DoorDash is going to be sorry it ever treated you like shit. I can guarantee that."

I hung up and took a deep breath, trying to steady my racing heartbeat. I opened the door and was shocked to see what looked like tears in Dane's bright blue eyes. I sighed. He clearly didn't understand what I was trying to do. He hadn't heard the whole conversation, and he didn't realize talking to me was the best thing that could have happened to this customer service representative. I was going to save him. If only Dane could understand that, I knew he'd be proud of me. But that was the problem; he just didn't understand.

CHAPTER 11

THE BREAKDOWN

It was two in the morning, and I was feeling desperate. Wells had been asleep for three hours. Our pediatrician had said he could go up to four hours in between feedings, since he was nearly back to his birth weight. Dane said he would rather wake Wells at the three-hour mark to be on the safe side, but his position was making me panic. The pediatrician had said Wells was strong enough to sleep four hours. Why was Dane insisting we disobey the pediatrician's recommendations? What if waking Wells up after only three hours instead of four meant he wouldn't get enough rest? We might stunt his growth. He might fail to meet his milestones. I was determined to protect Wells from Dane's refusal to do what the pediatrician said.

I was beginning to suspect something was wrong with Dane. He seemed much more stressed than I had expected. Dane had always been the calmer of the two of us; nothing rattled him. But he was unraveling under the strains of new parenthood, and I was starting to worry about his mental state. The stress appeared to be impairing his ability to think clearly. What else could explain his refusal to follow the pediatrician's instructions?

"Let's just wake him now and you can feed him. We're awake anyway," said Dane.

"No!" My voice came out surprisingly shrill. "Dr. Jackson said to let him sleep four hours! You're going to sleep deprive him!"

My heart started to race. What was going on here? Was Dane having some sort of stress-induced mental breakdown? Why couldn't he just do what the doctor said? Why was he insisting on putting our baby in danger? I needed to do something, and fast.

"I'm going to call Lucas," I announced.

Lucas was one of our friends from college and an anesthesiologist. When I was pregnant, I had asked Lucas all about epidurals, and he had assured me I could call him any time with questions. I decided to take him up on his offer.

"Jessica, no. It's two in the morning." Dane reached for my phone, but I snatched it away from him.

"I don't care. This is an emergency." I turned back to my phone and searched for Lucas's number.

Dane dropped his head into his hands. He really was having some sort of breakdown, I thought. I just hoped Lucas could talk some sense into him.

"Hello?" Lucas's voice sounded scratchy. I could tell I had woken him up, but I rushed right into my questions. Dane was falling apart, and I didn't have any time to waste.

"Lucas, I'm so sorry for calling you this late, but there's an emergency," I said. "At Wells's four-day appointment, our pediatrician said we should let him sleep up to four hours in between feedings. He's only been sleeping for three hours, and Dane wants to wake him up already. In your professional opinion, do you think that's dangerous?" I waited for Lucas to confirm my suspicions. Surely he would side with me. I was the sane one managing to keep my wits about me amid all the stress, while Dane was floundering.

The line was silent. "Are you asking whether it's dangerous to wake a baby up after three hours instead of four?" Lucas sounded confused.

"Yes," I said impatiently.

I was surprised that Lucas seemed to be struggling with the question. He was a highly trained medical professional, and the answer seemed obvious. What was the issue? I must have woken him up in the middle of a REM cycle and his brain was foggy as a result.

"I don't want to wake Wells up yet because he's not going to get enough sleep. He needs to get enough rest, and Dane is refusing to listen to our doctor. I don't know what's going on with him, but he doesn't seem to be able to think clearly right now." I shot a look at Dane, who still had his head in his hands.

"I think the difference between sleeping for three hours versus four isn't that significant," Lucas said.

I was stunned. Had everyone around me gone crazy? Why wasn't anyone concerned about Wells's well-being?

"Thanks so much for talking to us this late, Lucas. We're going to let you get back to sleep," Dane said, reaching for my phone again.

"No!" I leaped backward out of his reach. "Lucas, I'm sorry, but I still have more questions. We have another appointment with the pediatrician in a few days. Do you really think it's safe to let him sleep for only three hours at a time until then? What kind of damage could a lack of sleep over the next few days do?"

Lucas hesitated. "If you're worried about Wells's sleep, you should really talk to your doctor about it. In the meantime, you can just let him sleep for four hours in between feedings if that's what you're more comfortable with."

"I told you!" I said triumphantly to Dane. "We should let him sleep four hours. Lucas just said so."

Dane sighed. "Thanks, Lucas. We really appreciate your help, and we're going to let you go now."

I felt confident I had gotten the answer I needed. "Yes, Lucas, thanks so much for talking to us about this. You're the best." I hung up the phone and smiled at Dane. "See? We should let Wells sleep another hour, just like Lucas said."

Dane rubbed his temples. "That's not what he said, Jessica. He said eating every three or four hours is fine, and we should do what we're comfortable with. Wells's stomach is tiny and can't hold much at a time. Let's just wake him up and feed him so we can be sure he's getting enough."

Cold tendrils of panic began to shoot up from my stomach. What was happening to Dane? Even after talking to Lucas, he was still refusing to follow Dr. Jackson's instructions. He had developed some sort of obsession with feeding Wells every three hours. Was this the beginning of a breakdown? Was Dane even capable of rational thought anymore? Were Wells and I safe?

I ran to our room and shut myself in our walk-in closet. I needed to think, but my mind was spiraling. Were Wells and I in danger? It didn't seem like Dane was able to think clearly anymore. The stress of parenting had made him snap, and now it was all up to me to keep Wells safe. I needed to get us out of the house.

I picked up my phone with trembling fingers and called my friend Katie. Katie and her husband Kyle were good friends of ours who lived in the neighborhood. Wells and I would be safe with them.

The phone rang several times before Katie picked up. She sounded groggy.

"Katie, I'm so sorry to call you this late, but it's an emergency." My voice trembled, and I struggled to steady it. "I can't believe this is happening, but Dane is having some kind of mental breakdown. I don't know if it's safe for Wells and I to be here." I explained everything about what Dr. Jackson and Lucas had said, and how Dane had become dangerously obsessed with feeding Wells every three hours, even though it meant depriving him of sleep.

Katie listened without interrupting. "I can tell you're upset," she said slowly. "What exactly makes you feel like you're not safe at home?"

I tried to swallow the lump of cold, hard fear in my throat. "I feel like Dane is losing his mind. I don't know what he's capable of right now. It's so scary. This is when I'm supposed to be able to rely on him, and he's completely falling apart." I began to sob.

It was so unfair. I had given birth just ten days ago. I was still layering ice pads and absorbent liners in my underwear and constantly adjusting myself when I sat down to avoid soreness. Dane was supposed to be taking care of me, not making me call our friend in the middle of the night to come and pick me up. One of the things I loved most about Dane was his dependability. If he said he would do something, I could always consider it done. But here he was, falling to pieces when I needed him the most.

"So can you come get me?" I managed to choke out through my tears. "I can pack a bag and wait outside for you." I shivered at the thought of waiting outside in the February night air, but it was what the situation demanded.

It seemed to take Katie ages to respond. "I think leaving in the middle of the night might make things worse. That would be really stressful for Dane."

I considered this. Katie was a smart person, and I trusted her judgment, but things had gone downhill so fast that I didn't know what to think anymore.

"What about first thing in the morning?" I asked. "Maybe you could come at six?" I checked my watch. It was 2:24 a.m. I felt reasonably confident I could keep Wells and myself safe from Dane and his instability for just a few hours. Once we were safe at Katie and Kyle's, I'd be able to think more clearly and I could decide what to do. It was obvious that I needed to get Dane help, but I wasn't sure what kind.

A wave of resentment washed over me. I was supposed to be focusing on my recovery, not finding help for other people. Didn't I deserve even a few weeks of focusing on myself? But clearly, the answer was no. Here I was, in the middle of the night, being forced to beg a friend to come rescue me and try to figure out what to do about my husband's debilitated mental state.

"Let's talk again in a few hours after you've gotten some rest. If you still feel unsafe tomorrow morning, we'll come and get you," Katie said.

I breathed a sigh of relief. "Thank you, Katie. I mean it. I can't believe I have to ask this of you, but I wouldn't do it unless it was an emergency. I hope you know that," I sniffled into the phone, wiping my nose.

"I know," Katie said gently. "Why don't you lie down for a bit? You must be so tired."

"Okay, I will," I said. "I'll call you in a few hours."

I hung up and looked down at my hands, which were trembling violently. I clenched them into fists and tried to calm my ragged breath. I had no intention of lying down. Despite not having slept all day, I wasn't the least bit tired. My mind was racing with all the things I needed to do. Pack a bag for myself. Gather all of Wells's things and bring his car seat inside. Figure out how to get Dane professional help. My mind stuck on the last item. It was so incredibly unfair. I had so much going on. It wasn't right for me to have to worry about Dane too. Suddenly, I had an idea.

I picked up my phone and called Dane's dad. When he answered, I didn't even bother to say hello.

"Eric, I need your help. Something is wrong with Dane, and I don't have the capacity to deal with it." My words came tumbling out of my mouth. "He's losing his damn mind at the worst possible time." Anger began to billow in my chest. "I don't know if he needs therapy, or meds, or to go to the hospital, and I shouldn't be the one to have to figure it out." I could feel myself getting more and more worked up at the injustice of it all. I could no longer moderate my voice. I started to yell. "I can't believe he's choosing right now to fall apart. I just gave birth in the middle of a fucking pandemic. I've got enough going on without having to worry about Dane too. I need to be focused on myself and Wells and nothing else. He needs to get his fucking act together!"

Dane and my mom had begun whispering urgently outside the bedroom door, but I ignored them. I needed Eric to jump into action. I couldn't be the only grown-up in the room who was managing to hold it all together. I needed someone else on my team.

"You need to do something, Eric. I don't know what, but I need you to figure it out and then do it. I can't handle this all on my own. Dane has completely abandoned me, and I need him to get the fuck over himself and come back to reality. I need my fucking husband back!" My heart was beating heavily against my rib cage, and my entire body was trembling. But it felt good to finally ask for what I needed. I was so used to taking care of everyone else, but it was my turn to be selfish. Someone else was going to have to swoop in and save the day for once.

"So, can I count on you to fix this?" I demanded.

"You don't have to worry. Everything is going to be fine." Eric's voice sounded unnaturally slow. Was he somehow failing to grasp that this was an emergency? Why wasn't he springing into action as the situation warranted?

"I need you to fucking do something, Eric! Your son is falling the fuck apart, and I need you to do something!" I was screaming now. "Do you get it? Do you hear me? *Do something!*" My voice was beginning to feel hoarse.

I could hear Dane in the hallway, louder now. I heard him say "mental health crisis" and "emergency." I threw the door open and saw Dane on the phone. "What are you doing? Who are you talking to?" I demanded.

Dane didn't answer, and instead turned and hurried down the hallway. I tried to follow him, but my mom blocked my way.

"Who are you talking to?" I yelled over my mom's shoulder.

I heard Dane giving the person on the other end of the line our address and asking them to hurry.

"Are you calling 911? Are you kidding me? You're the one losing your fucking mind and you're calling 911 on *me*? No! I'm calling 911 on *you*!"

I raced back down the hallway to our bedroom and slammed the door behind me. What the hell was going on? Was I in some sort of twisted alternate reality? My husband was falling to pieces before my very eyes, and now on top of everything he had somehow convinced himself that I was the one with the problem?

I locked myself in our bathroom and dialed 911. My hands were shaking so badly I could barely press the numbers. When the dispatcher answered, I told her my husband was having a mental health crisis and I needed her to send someone immediately.

"Are you safe right now?" the dispatcher asked.

I checked the knob to make sure the door was locked. "Yes. I'm locked in a bathroom."

"All right, ma'am. Are you able to stay there until the paramedics arrive?"

"Yes." My teeth were starting to chatter. What had happened to my picture-perfect life?

The dispatcher confirmed my address and assured me help was on the way. She stayed on the line with me until I could hear the paramedics knocking on our front door. I heard my mother let them in. A few moments later, there was a firm knock on the bathroom door.

"Jessica? My name is Mike, and I'm here to help you. Can you please open the door?"

I felt a rush of relief. Dane would get the help he needed and was going to return to his normal, steadfast self. I opened the door.

"Hi there, Jessica. It's nice to meet you." Mike offered me a kind smile. "Can you tell me a little bit about why you called us out tonight?"

A second paramedic stood behind Mike, and I could hear a third in the hall. Everything would be okay. The professionals were here, and I was safe. I took a deep breath to steady myself.

"I just had a baby ten days ago, and something happened to my husband. He's normally really calm and rational, but he's been under a lot of stress ever since he burned the pacifiers and put us all in danger. He's acting crazy, he's not listening to our pediatrician, and I think our son might be in danger." I shuddered. "I can't believe this is happening. It's completely unlike him. I never in a million years would have thought he'd fall apart like this."

Mike nodded. "It sounds like you're dealing with a lot. We're going to get you some help though, so don't worry. I think it would be best if you came to the hospital with us. Is that okay with you?"

So it had come to this. Dane's mental state had deteriorated so completely that he needed to be hospitalized. I couldn't believe that my husband—my smart, thoughtful, even-tempered husband—was on his way to a psych ward after less than two weeks as a parent. But Mike was the expert, and I trusted him. If he thought Dane needed to go to the hospital, then that's what we'd do.

Mike and the other paramedic stepped into the hallway so I could get dressed. I had been wearing my bathrobe when they arrived. I walked around our room in a daze, getting yoga pants out of a drawer and pulling a thick sweatshirt over my head. I caught a glance of myself in the full-length mirror on the back of our door and saw my eyes were puffy from crying and my cheeks were blotchy. I couldn't believe what Dane was putting me through. Maybe parenthood wasn't going to be so easy after all.

CHAPTER 12

INTAKE

Mike sat with me in the back of the ambulance. I was surprised Dane wasn't with us, but I reasoned they must have driven him in a separate ambulance. We probably had to go into the emergency room through separate entrances, since he was the patient and I was his support system. On the short ride to the hospital, I told Mike the abbreviated version of what had happened.

"I just never thought he'd fall apart like this," I said, fighting back tears.

"I know things seem hard right now, but they're going to be okay," Mike assured me.

I nodded. I wanted so badly to believe him.

We pulled up to the side entrance of the emergency room, and Mike led me inside. Dane was nowhere in sight. Maybe he was already in one of the examination rooms. We went into a large room with stark white walls on three sides and thick panes of glass on the fourth. A nurse stepped inside and shut the door behind her, drawing a curtain across the glass. She handed me a hospital gown and asked me to get changed. I stared at her.

"Is this really necessary?" I asked. "I understand you're probably just trying to keep Dane calm since he thinks I'm the one having some sort of episode, but do I really need to wear a hospital gown?"

The nurse smiled at me sympathetically. Her badge identified her as Erin. "We really do need you to get changed," she said.

I didn't want to be difficult. These people were trying to help Dane, and I didn't want to get in the way of that. I changed my clothes without further complaint and went to sit on one of the chairs in the corner.

"Actually, you can have a seat on the table," Erin said, gesturing to the paper-covered examination table.

"Really? Why?" I was baffled. The staff was starting to take things too far. I understood the need to keep Dane from getting hysterical, but the charade of putting me on an exam table in a hospital gown struck me as a bridge too far. Surely they didn't need to go to these lengths to keep Dane from breaking down even further. Where was he, anyway? He wasn't even around to see me in my hospital gown costume, so what was the point?

"It would just be best to have you up on the table," Erin said.

I furrowed my brow but complied. Erin took my blood pressure and made a note on her clipboard. I appreciated that she was taking the time to make sure the stress of Dane's mental collapse wasn't taking a toll on me physically. Elevated blood pressure in the postpartum period could be incredibly dangerous.

"My colleague, Shannon, will be right in to talk to you," Erin said, pulling open the curtain and leaving me alone in the room.

What an incredibly bizarre situation this was becoming. These people were the experts, but I didn't see how any of this patient role-playing was going to help Dane.

Shannon entered the room a few minutes later and took a seat in a chair across from the exam table.

"Hi, Jessica. It's nice to meet you," Shannon said. She smiled kindly, and I liked her immediately. Dane would be in good hands with her.

"I understand you just had a baby," Shannon said.

I nodded. "His name is Wells. He's ten days old."

"Wow, such a little guy. Can you tell me about him?"

I smiled. "He's the snuggliest little burrito. He has a ton of dark hair, and he loves being swaddled. We've got a swaddle with giraffes on it that's his favorite. And he doesn't cry unless he's tired or hungry. He's a really chill baby."

"He sounds adorable," Shannon said. "And how have you been sleeping?"

"Not much, to be honest. But I don't need it. I'm weirdly never tired. I always heard that being a new mom was exhausting, but it's not at all. I actually feel way more energized than I did when I was pregnant."

Shannon nodded, but I thought she looked a bit concerned. "How has your mood been?" she asked. "Any changes you've noticed? Any anger or irritability?"

I thought back to the night I had yelled at Dane when he came upstairs to tell me it was time to feed Wells. I still didn't remember exactly what I'd been upset at him about, but I knew I had raised my voice, which was very unlike me.

"There was one night when I yelled at my husband," I admitted. "I was picking up the kitchen and having some alone time and he interrupted me to ask me to feed our son. I got frustrated and yelled."

"What's your relationship normally like with your husband? Does it tend to have a lot of conflict?"

I shook my head. "It's the opposite. We never yell. He's usually very calm and level-headed. That's why it's been such a shock to see him having this breakdown. He used to be my rock." I could feel tears starting to prick my eyes. "I'm going to have to come to terms with the fact that I can't fully rely on him anymore. He's more fragile than I realized."

Shannon set her clipboard in her lap and looked at me closely. "Let's talk more about your husband's condition. Can you walk me through exactly why you called 911?"

"I was worried my husband was putting our son in danger. Our pediatrician said Wells could sleep up to four hours in between feedings, but Dane was insisting we wake him up after only three. He was obsessed with waking him up early, and I got worried about the sleep deprivation. It's not like Dane to just ignore what a doctor says. It would only make sense if he was having some sort of breakdown. And if he was having a breakdown, then Wells and I weren't safe, so I called for help."

"Thank you for explaining that to me," Shannon said gently. "I'm going to go have a talk with the doctor, and then he'll be in to see you." Shannon gave me one last smile before she left the room. I thought I detected a hint of sadness in her eyes. It must have been hard for her to hear about a husband and father essentially abandoning his family when they needed him most.

I watched Shannon walk past a row of desks and stop to speak to a man in a white coat, who I assumed was the doctor. Then I saw Dane walk toward them. He was still in his street clothes. I was confused. Why hadn't they done intake with him yet? Why wasn't he in his hospital gown? The charade of me playing the patient while Dane was allowed to think he was the support person was going much too far.

I pressed my ear against the glass in an effort to hear what Dane, Shannon, and the doctor were saying, but they were too far away and the glass was too thick. I tried to open the door and was taken aback when I found it was locked. Why had they locked me in this room? Did they think Dane might try to attack me? He was in the middle of a mental health crisis, to be sure, but I felt confident he'd never try to hurt me. The hospital staff had gotten it all wrong. I wanted to tell them that, but I was trapped in the room.

A thought occurred to me. What if they were testing me to see whether I was a competent caretaker for Dane before they let him go home with me? What if they were watching me to see how hard I would fight to try to get to him? I looked around the room for a camera. Maybe I was being watched by someone in a central command center. I didn't see any cameras, but that didn't mean they weren't there. They were probably tucked under the ceiling tiles to avoid being spotted.

I stood in the middle of the room and spun slowly to direct my voice into each corner, not knowing which one contained the hidden camera. "Hello to whoever is watching this. Do I just need to ask you to unlock the door? Is that how this works?" I paused, waiting to hear a response or a clicking as the door unlocked. Nothing happened. "I need to be with my husband right now. He's going through something serious, and I don't think it's helpful to keep me away from him." Still no response. I decided to try the door again.

I turned the knob and tried to open the door, but it stayed firmly in place. Maybe it was jammed. I gave it a gentle shove with my shoulder. It didn't budge. I threw my weight against the door, but it refused to open.

I looked at the people on the other side of the door. They were typing at computers and carrying file folders around. Everyone looked like they were moving in slow motion. Were they actors? Maybe their slow movements were meant to be soothing to Dane and help him calm down. The woman sitting at the computer closest to me was typing comically slowly. Was she even typing real sentences? Maybe she was just pushing keyboard buttons at random.

And then it hit me. I must be in an escape room. That would explain why I was locked in a room with a camera in the ceiling. The game master must be watching me from a control booth, ready to step in and give me clues if it appeared that I was stuck. I breathed a sigh of relief. I loved escape rooms. I had played one not so long ago at an annual trademark lawyers' conference in Boston. A few of my colleagues and I had taken in-house counsel for some of our clients and done an ancient civilization-themed escape room. The clues included maps and hieroglyphics and hidden rooms. It had been a great bonding activity. We had broken off into groups and each tackled different puzzles within the room, reporting back to the group triumphantly when we cracked a code. We ended up making it out of the room with two minutes to spare. We giddily rehashed our victory over dinner later that night and agreed it was one of the best outings we'd ever had at the yearly conference.

There must be clues hidden in the room.

I spun around, surveying my surroundings. There wasn't much to see. The exam table and a small metal table and two chairs were the only furnishings in the room. Maybe there was a key to the door secured to one of the pieces of furniture. I got on my hands and knees, wincing from the pain in my pelvis, and looked under the metal table and chairs, but saw nothing. Then I lifted the paper cover off the exam table and searched it, to no avail. I was stumped. Where else could a clue be hiding?

I turned my attention back to the camera in the ceiling. "Can I get a clue, please?" I asked.

In the other escape rooms I'd played, if you got stuck and needed help getting to the next step, the game master would give you a clue on a screen or through an intercom. I waited, but no clue was given. I looked back at the door and saw Dane, Shannon, and the doctor were on their way over. Maybe they wanted my help doing some sort of intervention with Dane. I wondered if he had resisted their attempts to help him, and that was why he hadn't gotten changed into his hospital gown yet.

They came inside and shut the door behind them. Dane had tears in his eyes. "Can we sit?" He motioned to the exam table.

"Of course," I said, taking a seat on the crinkly paper. I draped my arms around his neck. "I know this is hard, but we're going to get through it. I love you."

Dane pulled away and looked at me hard. "I love you too. I love you so much." His voice was shaking. He must have been scared about what was happening to him. Being self-aware enough to realize your sanity is slipping must be terrifying. I was determined to be his rock.

Shannon and the doctor, who introduced himself as Dr. Harrison, sat down in the two chairs across from us. Dr. Harrison asked me about my pregnancy and delivery and how I had been doing since we brought Wells home. I thought it was polite of him to ask but wondered why he was focusing on me and not Dane. I was starting to find this charade of playing the patient myself to be baffling. What could be the benefit of keeping up the ruse this long?

Then Dr. Harrison looked at me directly and asked, "Why do you think we're here, Jessica?"

I sighed. "Dane is having a mental health crisis. He's losing touch with reality, and I was scared that Wells and I might be in danger, so I called 911." I reached over and grabbed Dane's hand. "I don't think Dane would ever hurt me, and never on purpose, but I needed to make sure Wells was safe, so I had to call." I squeezed Dane's hand. I hoped he would forgive me for reporting him to the authorities.

Dr. Harrison turned to Dane. "And Dane, why do you think we're here?"

Dane took a deep breath. "A few days after we got home from the hospital, Jessica started acting strangely. She's been yelling and not sleeping and saying a lot of things that don't make sense. I'm worried she's having some kind of psychotic episode."

I shook my head. "Do you see what I mean?" I asked Dr. Harrison. "He's losing his mind."

Dr. Harrison paused, then fixed his gaze on me and said gently, "We're here because of you."

A panicked sensation crashed over me. Had I heard Dr. Harrison correctly? Was this some sort of terrible joke? "What do you mean?" I demanded. My palm suddenly felt clammy against Dane's skin, and I could feel my pulse accelerate.

"You're going to need to spend some time in the hospital. You're in good hands, and you're going to be just fine. We'll get you home to your baby as fast as we can."

I was stunned. Had Dane tricked Dr. Harrison into thinking I was the one who needed help? I had explained everything that had happened with the burning pacifiers and Dane's inability to follow the pediatrician's instructions to Shannon, and again to Dr. Harrison, but somehow they failed to understand Dane was the one who needed to stay in the hospital.

"Why don't you take a minute to say good-bye to Dane, and then we're going to help you get some sleep," Dr. Harrison said. He and Shannon got up and stepped outside, leaving Dane and I alone.

Dane wrapped me in his arms and pressed my head against his shoulder. "We're going to get through this. I promise." His voice quivered. For a moment, I was too shocked to speak. How had this happened? I had a ten-day-old baby at home, and I was about to be locked up in a hospital. Was something actually wrong with me? What was going on?

I pulled back and looked at Dane. "I don't understand what's happening." My eyes started to water. "Do I really need to stay here?"

Dane swallowed hard and nodded. "But not for long. They're going to help you get stable and then you can come home and start therapy. There's a spot for you in the intensive outpatient group as soon as you're home."

My thoughts had begun racing so quickly I could hardly focus on what Dane was saying. Had a mere ten days of motherhood made me go crazy? What kind of mother needed to be hospitalized after being with her baby for less than two weeks? How on Earth had I ended up in this position? I clung to Dane and began to cry. I suddenly felt terrified. I had a baby, and it broke me. What did that say about my capacity to be a good mother to Wells? What if the hospital couldn't fix me and I was broken forever?

Dr. Harrison and Shannon came back into the room.

"Alright, Jessica, it's time to get you some sleep, and then we can take you up to your room," Dr. Harrison said.

Dane cupped my face in his hands and looked at me with teary eyes. "We're going to get through this together. We're a team. I love you so much." He kissed my forehead and got up from the exam table, folding his coat over his arm. Then he was gone, and I found myself sitting in a hospital gown that grazed my swollen postpartum stomach, getting a shot that made me sleep for the first time in days.

CHAPTER 13

SUPER SAD UNICORN

It was nearly lunchtime on Sunday when I arrived on the sixteenth floor. My room was surprisingly spacious, with built-in shelves, a bathroom with an opaque plastic curtain instead of a door, and a view that included my home, five blocks to the east. It was both comforting and maddening to be able to see my house but not be allowed to go back to it. No one told me how long I needed to stay in the hospital, and they found ways to sidestep the question when I asked.

The other frustrating thing was no one told me the therapy schedule. Surely my days would be filled with doctors and counselors working feverishly to get me back to Wells. But why hadn't the nurse told me anything about them when she deposited me in my room? Why hadn't anyone told me how this place worked?

I put my mask on and stepped into the hallway. The tile felt hard and unforgiving under my sock-clad feet. My winter boots were stored in a locker outside my room that I didn't have access to. I began slowly walking down the hallway. Each room I passed contained a patient in a blue, open-backed hospital gown. They were all lying on their sides facing away from me. One patient had a giant tattoo that consumed his entire back. Why was everyone seemingly asleep in the middle of the day? And why were they all laying in the same position?

I had a thought. The reason no one had told me about a therapy schedule and I was the only one out wandering the hallway was that this was some sort of specialized therapy program just for me. The "patients" in the other rooms were all actors. It was one of those strange gigs actors took when they were between theater roles and looking for a day job as a barista or waiter. It was like when I took a deposition training class and the instructors brought in out-of-work actors to play the parts of hostile witnesses. The actors were instructed to be difficult and obstructionistic when responding to our questions so we could practice using different techniques to get the testimony we wanted. I suspected a similar situation here. The staff must have told these people to interact with me in specific ways as part of my therapy. They were all lying in bed pretending to be asleep because their parts didn't call for them to speak to me yet. Surely they'd all come to life soon.

I went back to my room and waited for lunch. I put my foot up on my windowsill and stretched my hamstrings and obliques. It felt good to move my body. I brought my foot back down to the ground and began brushing it backward and forward like a ballerina standing at a barre. I did a few deep knee bends. Maybe there would be a ballet class as part of my therapy. Movement and music both had therapeutic effects—although I had never been a big fan of ballet. During my time as a competitive figure skater, my coach insisted I take ballet classes as part of my off-ice training. She said it would help with my posture and flexibility, but I found it painfully boring. Standing at the barre and practicing first, second, and third positions over and over again, all I wanted to do was get back out on the ice. Ballet wouldn't be my first choice for a movement therapy class, but, obviously, there was no ice rink in the hospital, so I understood if ballet was the next best thing the counselors could offer me.

A nurse knocked on my doorframe and told me it was time for lunch. I thanked her and began to follow her down the hall to the dayroom where meals were served. "Don't forget your mask," she told me.

I went back to my room and hooked the loops of the surgical mask over my ears. A year into the pandemic, I still wasn't used to wearing a mask. Since I got pregnant two months after the virus turned everyone's lives upside down, I had been mostly quarantined for the past nine months. I was terrified of contracting COVID-19 while pregnant. Everything was so uncertain, and no one knew what kinds of disastrous effects the virus might have on developing fetuses. I rarely left the house or saw anyone other than Dane, so wearing a mask was largely unnecessary.

Some of the only times I had ventured outside were to see my ob-gyn, always alone since partners were no longer allowed inside the office. I was alone the first time I heard Wells's heartbeat and alone the first time I saw him on a sonogram. It was so different from my first pregnancy, when Dane giddily joined me at the appointment to confirm there was, indeed, a human beginning to take form inside of me. But shortly after that euphoric doctor's visit, the cramps came, then the blood, then the late-night call to the doctor's emergency off-hours line. And then the baby was gone. Already more than eight weeks along, I was forced to have the remains of my first baby vacuumed out of my traitorous body. I hated my body for failing at one of the most primal elements of womanhood. The only good thing was that I had

Dane at my side while the last traces of what should have been the start of our new family were taken away from me. The pandemic struck less than a month later.

I walked into the dayroom and saw three other patients in blue gowns sitting at small tables with trays of food in front of them. No one was speaking. A nurse handed me a small slip of paper and a marker and told me to pick what I wanted for lunch. I scanned the choices and immediately started laughing.

Someone clearly designed this menu to get a smile out of me during a stressful time. Dane must have given the nurses the information they needed to craft the menu. There was an extensive list of condiments; Dane constantly teased me for how I tended to eat things plain without any accompaniments. I was the only person I knew who didn't put ketchup or mustard on my burgers. One of the beverage options was Crystal Light, but the trademark registration symbol was missing. Dane, of course, knew that as a trademark lawyer it was a pet peeve of mine when registration symbols were missing. One of the available side dishes was mixed vegetables. The day before I was brought to the hospital, my mom and I had been reminiscing about how my Colombian grandmother had been horrified by the frozen veggie medleys with carrots, peas, and corn that most American families ate in the '90s. Laughing with my mother had been a happy moment that Dane must have told the nurses about.

The nurse returned and collected my menu and marker. A man in his fifties wearing wire-rimmed glasses, who had been sitting at the table behind me, asked if he could join me. I eagerly agreed; I found the silence in the dayroom unsettling.

"I'm David," he said. "I'd shake your hand, but we're not supposed to touch in here."

I nodded. "You can tell me what all the rules are. No one's told me anything so far. They haven't even told me when therapy starts."

David cocked his head. "There's no therapy here. This is it." He gestured around the room.

I was confused. "So we do the therapy ourselves? Like, patients counseling other patients?"

David shrugged. "I guess you could say that."

Maybe I wasn't surrounded by actors after all. Maybe we were all just trying to get out of this hospital but needed to figure out the key to our freedom on our own. And then I remembered; I was in an escape room. The special menu must have been one of the clues. All the patients must be playing their own individualized versions of the escape room. We all needed to solve our individual puzzles before we would be released.

The nurse returned with my lunch tray: chicken fingers, a roll, carrots and celery, and a fruit cup. I appreciated that chicken fingers, one of my comfort foods, had been included in my menu on the first day.

"Have you been here long?" I asked David, spearing a grape and a piece of cantaloupe.

"A few days," David said. "But I've been here before."

"Really?"

"Yeah. Usually around the same time every year, on the anniversary. Something bad happened."

I didn't ask for details, not wanting to pry.

"Last year I got put in Lakeshore," he said. "Have you ever been there?"

I shook my head. "What's Lakeshore?"

"It's the worst. It's like this place, but tenfold. They torture you. There's some real padded-wall shit going on. Trust me, you don't want to end up there." His eyes were unnaturally wide and unblinking.

I shuddered at the thought of being locked up again. "I believe you."

"So what do you do when you're not trapped in this place?" David asked. "I'm a professor."

"I'm a lawyer. I work at a boutique IP firm. I've been there my whole career."

David raised his eyebrows. "A lawyer? You're fancy. There are never any fancy people in here other than me. You're like a unicorn."

I snorted. "Yeah. A super sad unicorn locked in a psych ward with a ten-day-old baby at home."

David raised his eyebrows again. "You just had a baby?"

I patted my bloated postpartum belly. "Yeah. His name is Wells. I had a baby, and apparently it made me crazy. I thought my husband was having some kind of mental health crisis. I called 911, but when we got here the doctors said it was because of me."

David gave me a long look. "I don't think you're crazy. I think this place is crazy. They force a bunch of drugs on you and there are guards and some of the people who work here are evil. Real sick fucks. You can tell by the nail polish."

"Nail polish?"

"Yeah. The good ones always wear nail polish. It's their way of letting us know we're safe with them. It's the ones without the nail polish you have to watch out for. If somebody ever tries to sedate you, it'll be one of those fuckers without any nail polish. You'll see."

I glanced down at my own chipped polish and thought about the nurse who had delivered my lunch. Were her nails painted? I couldn't remember. What if she was one of the bad ones? What if she had snuck something into my food? I began feeling queasy.

"You've got to really watch the meds they give you too," David continued. "Make them show you the labels of everything. Sometimes they try to slip you extra shit so you get all loopy and can't remember what they've done to you. It's messed up."

I could feel my fingertips and the insides of my wrists starting to tingle like they did when I was about to have a panic attack. My body had just gone through the most revelatory thing that would ever happen to it, and instead of recovering at home I was in this unsettling, apparently dangerous place, filled with people who may or may not be actors and a set of rules for getting out I didn't understand. I began to cry.

An older Black man who had been sitting alone at a table in the back of the room got up and walked over. He put his hands on the back of the chair across from me. "Hi there, baby girl. Mind if I sit down?" he asked.

I shook my head. Maybe he was one of the other patients who was supposed to be serving as my therapist. Maybe he had the next clue for how I could get out of this place.

"I'm Isaiah," he said, pulling out the chair. "It sounds to me like you're having a hard time."

I nodded, wiping my nose with the back of my hand. My ID bracelet slipped down my wrist and I looked at the admission date: 2/21/21. It sounded like it should have been a magical date. But instead, it was a reminder that exactly ten days with my baby had somehow broken me.

"You're going to be just fine. Your spirit just got a little out of whack is all. It's easy to happen in this world we live in." Isaiah gave me a gentle smile.

I sniffled. "Something is wrong with me. I don't know what's happening with my brain. I had a baby, and everything just fell apart. My thoughts are always racing. I can't focus on anything, and I keep getting confused. I get angry really quickly. I don't even recognize myself."

Isaiah reached across the table and grabbed my hands. "You're going through a lot, mama. Motherhood is a wonderful gift from God, but it's also full of trials and tribulations. What you've got to do is put your faith in Him. You know what I'm talking about?"

"I'm not a religious person anymore," I said. Although at that moment I desperately wished I still was. I would have loved nothing more than to have said a prayer and had the luxury of believing it would fix everything. I wanted to outsource the resolution of all my problems to a higher power and trust that everything would turn out fine if I just believed. But I didn't have it in me.

I vividly remembered what it was like to pray for a sign to guide my decisions and to firmly believe one would be forthcoming. I prayed about which college to attend and whether I should leave my perfect-on-paper college boyfriend to be with Dane, who was my opposite in so many ways. I prayed that Whitney wouldn't go to hell after she killed herself, and I prayed for relief from the crippling panic attacks that seized me in the wake of her death. But that time in my life was behind me. I was on my own now.

"Have you thought about welcoming God back into your heart?" asked Isaiah. "I know He'd love to have you back in His flock. He's whispering in my ear right now about how much He's missed you. You're one of His beloved children."

A nurse came over to our table and asked Isaiah to let go of my hands. "You know we don't allow touching."

Isaiah put his hands in the air. "My apologies, ma'am. I'm just trying to minister to a lost daughter of God."

The nurse smiled tightly. "Let's just keep the ministry verbal."

Out of the corner of my eye, I saw David snicker and cross his arms. Something told me he was as distant from God as I was.

Isaiah turned his attention back to me. "Everything you're going through would be so much easier if you let God walk the path with you. I'm speaking from experience here. I sit before you a changed man. I was an addict for years. The only thing I cared about was where I was going to get my next hit."

"I hear you on that one," said David.

"My man here understands," said Isaiah. "I was at the bottom of a dark pit, and it seemed like there was no way out. But then God reached out His ever-loving hands and pulled me up. I didn't deserve it, I didn't earn it, but He did it anyway. Because our God is a loving God who adores you no matter what you've done. He just wants you to adore Him back."

"If He's so adoring, then what the fuck are we all doing here?" asked David. "What kind of god lets people be locked up in an insane asylum when they didn't even do anything wrong?" He gestured at me. "She's got a brand-new baby at home, and she's trapped in this hellhole. Why? What kind of god would let that happen?"

"My brother, that's where faith comes in. It's not always for us to know God's plan. We just have to trust that He has one."

"Oh yeah? Was it his plan for me to destroy Sylvia Plath's manuscripts? Because I did. That supposedly ever-loving god of yours let me go on such a bender that I ruined some of her most precious writings. The university trusted me with them, and I ripped them to shreds. We're never going to get them back, and I have to live with that. I'm a fucking monster. Your god let me be a monster."

"That's not God, my brother. That's Satan. Sometimes Satan wins the battle, but he'll never win the war. You can count on that. That's why you should join God's army. Fight on the side of goodness."

"No one in their right mind would let me into an army fighting for goodness. I already told you, I'm a monster."

"No one who repents for their sins is a monster. You're just a child of God who strayed from the flock and got lost on the path. God doesn't fault you for that. If you just accept Him, He'll accept you back."

Before David could respond, the nurse announced that everyone needed to return to their rooms for afternoon quiet time. Isaiah gave me a final, covert squeeze of the hand. "You're going to find your way back to God, mama. Welcome home."

I walked back to my room with my brain reeling. Did God really tell Isaiah that He missed me? Was all this my second clue? Did I need to rekindle my lost relationship with God before I could go home to Wells? I lay down on my bed and tried to focus my thoughts, but they galloped in all directions. Maybe I just needed to wait for a sign. If God really wanted me back, surely He'd let me know.

CHAPTER 14

ESCAPE ROOM THERAPY

I spent the afternoon quiet time trying to wrap my head around where I was and what I needed to do to gain my freedom. It seemed clear I was in some sort of cutting-edge, experimental therapy program. Because the program was tailored to me, it seemed to have aspects of improv comedy built in. There were no therapists and the patients had to counsel each other, much like participants in an improv scene have to work together to build a fictional world. Most of all, I felt certain the program was like an escape room, with clues I needed to solve to be released. It seemed to me that realizing the program was set up like an escape room was, in itself, the first challenge. I figured it out quickly. As David said, I was a unicorn. This place probably didn't get many law firm partners walking through its doors. I was clearly a special case.

But my fellow patients were probably each special in their own ways. They had been picked to be in the experimental program, after all. They must each have their own set of clues to conquer the escape room, and it was our collective job to help each other get out. I was determined to do my part.

When quiet time ended, I began walking back to the dayroom. On my way I passed a room with an abandoned lunch tray on the bed. I quickly stepped inside and read the menu on the tray. The patient had circled grape juice, animal crackers, and a turkey sandwich. These must be this person's special items, carefully selected to make them laugh and to give them a clue that they were participating in a therapeutic escape room. As I committed these items to memory, in case they were relevant to my own set of clues, a nurse beckoned me out of the room.

"There's no going into other patients' rooms, even when they're not there," she said.

I smiled. "Sorry, I forgot." I assumed she must have been instructed to act like a regular nurse to avoid giving away the escape room too easily. Surely she knew I was hunting for clues, and I wasn't really in trouble for going into the room. It was all just part of the game.

I proceeded to the dayroom, where I found David talking to a new patient. I decided to initiate an improv scene in case that was one of the steps to solving the escape room. I approached David's table, then nudged my mask underneath my nose to scratch an imaginary itch. I gasped and pulled my mask back up theatrically. "Oh my god, I'm so sorry!" I gushed to the new patient. "I didn't mean to expose you to COVID. That was so reckless of me. I can't believe I pulled my mask down within six feet of you!"

I turned frantically to David. "Was I within six feet of you? Did I just expose you? Oh my god, oh my god, oh my god." I began pacing back and forth in front of them, grabbing fistfuls of hair in my hands. I had expected them to pick up on the scene by now and jump in, but they were both just staring at me.

"Maybe I hadn't made it six feet from you yet. I was walking toward you, but I hadn't made it that far inside the door. I think I might have already pulled my mask back up by the time I got within six feet of you. No, no, that's not right. I was definitely just a few feet away from you when I did it. I'm horrible. If one of you gets COVID, I'll never forgive myself. What if you end up on oxygen? That doesn't just happen to smokers. It can happen to anyone!"

I paused to allow one of them to adopt their own character and join me in the scene. The new patient gave David an uncomfortable look, then said, "I don't think you need to worry. Pulling your mask down for a second isn't a big deal. We'll be fine."

He didn't stand up to join me or introduce any details that would tell me about his character or the fictional world we were supposed to be building together. I was disappointed he was being such a poor scene partner. Improv is all about "yes, and." You're supposed to build on what your scene partner has just said by adding new information that can be used to drive the scene. But this man gave me nothing to work with. Maybe he didn't yet realize we were in an experimental therapy program where we had to use improv skills to heal each other. I decided to abandon the scene and sat down a few tables away from David and the new patient to watch TV. The two of them resumed their conversation in low tones, too quiet for me to hear.

The show paused for an ad break, and a commercial for an office supply store began playing. A woman in a cardigan sat at a desktop computer with a man in a suit standing behind her, apparently dictating to her.

"Of course she's got to be the fucking secretary. They never let the woman put on a damn blazer and be the boss," I mumbled to the screen.

The next ad was for Old Navy. It featured a group of children ice skating on a frozen pond in thick mittens and pom-pom stocking caps. I gasped. These commercials had been selected especially for me.

I looked through the large window below the TV at the nurses hurrying around their station. One of them was watching the dayroom. She must have picked the ads when she saw me sit down in front of the TV, and they must be clues. The first ad was a nod to my staunch feminist side, and the second was about my love for figure skating. The nurses must have called Dane and asked him to describe me so they could select ads that would speak to me directly. Now I just needed to figure out what it all meant and how it could help me beat the escape room.

I cupped my chin in my hands and focused on the TV. The next ad was for a Ford truck. I burst out laughing, and David turned around to stare at me. My father hated Ford. He was a die-hard Chevy man. This ad was obviously meant to remind me of him.

My attention was pulled away from the TV by a woman in a blue hospital gown pacing uncertainly at the entrance to the dayroom.

"Do you want to come in?" I called to her. "You can sit with me."

She looked down at the floor and shuffled into the dayroom, taking the chair next to mine.

"I'm Jessica," I said.

"I'm Tiara," she whispered. She rested her hands on the table and I saw that the cuticle on her right thumb was ragged and bleeding. "I just got here."

I nodded. "It's kind of a weird place. We all have to pretend to be therapists to each other, and there are a bunch of clues. I just realized they pick the TV ads for us specifically, but I haven't figured out why yet." I turned my attention back to the TV, where a Snickers ad was playing. I couldn't think of any connection I had to Snickers. Maybe this ad was meant for Tiara.

"Does this ad mean anything to you? Does it remind you of anything?" I asked her.

Tiara frowned and shook her head. "I don't really like Snickers." She stared down at her hands. "The caramel is too sticky."

The ad must be directed at David or the new patient. But they weren't paying attention.

"Never mind then," I said. "Pay attention when you get your menus for meals tomorrow. They're going to have special items that are like inside jokes. Mine are Crystal Light and mixed veggies. Another guy has grape juice, turkey sandwiches, and animal crackers. Let me know once you see what yours are. I'm trying to figure out how the items lead us to the next clue."

Tiara nodded solemnly. "Okay. I'll pay attention."

I smiled, satisfied. "So where are you from? Do you live in the neighborhood?"

Tiara shook her head. "I just got to Chicago from Wisconsin." She stared down at her hands again. "My husband is a very bad man, and I had to get away. God told me to."

I frowned. "I'm sorry to hear that. It sounds really hard. I'm glad you're safe though."

"Not that safe," said David, repositioning his chair to face us. "I watched them tranq some guy yesterday. He was a little upset, but nothing major, and that big, burly nurse came over and jabbed him in the arm and took him to his room. I walked by a few minutes later and he was passed out. They'll take any excuse to knock you out around here. You have to be careful."

Tiara's eyes widened. "I don't want to get knocked out."

"Nobody does," said David. "But they don't care. We're not real humans to them. We're like broken little robots that they're trying to patch up just enough to be somewhat functional so they can send us back into the world where we're not their problem anymore."

I excused myself to go back to my room. I had only been in the ward for the afternoon, but I was already getting tired of David's rants. He didn't seem to appreciate the fact that we were in a special, experimental therapy program and not some generic psych ward. The treatment we were receiving was innovative and cutting-edge, yet all he could do was complain about it.

I sat down on the toilet and pulled down my postpartum mesh underwear. The pad inside was soaked in blood. I had expected to bleed while giving birth, but no one had prepared me for the amount of bleeding I'd still be doing several days after having Wells. I pulled the underwear back up and went into the hallway. I needed to load up on supplies. I made my way to the supply closet the nurse had shown me when I first arrived on the floor and felt my face flush when I saw one of the male security guards staffing it. I would have to ask this man for more mesh underwear and pads.

I was on my way back to my room, supplies in hand, when Tiara stopped me.

"I didn't get to ask you before. Can we please pray together? I'd really like it if you prayed with me."

I balked. I couldn't remember the last time I had prayed. It was probably during college, sometime after I'd given up on my church-finding mission. When my grandpa gave long, sometimes ostentatiously tearful prayers at Sunday night family dinners, I bowed my head, but let my mind go blank. I had no idea what to say to God. But Tiara seemed so lonely and fragile, and she was escaping such a bleak situation. I couldn't turn down her request.

We stood side by side with our backs against the wall and bowed our heads. Tiara clasped her hands in front of her chest and closed her eyes. "Dear Jesus, in your holy name I pray. I thank you for your guidance and your eternal love. I thank you for bringing Jessica into my life. We just met, but I believe you put her in my life for a reason, Lord. Please watch over her, and me, as we navigate this new place we have found ourselves in. Please help us learn the lessons we need to learn and better ourselves so we can be your representatives when we go out into the world. Thank you for your mercy and love, which I cherish every day. Amen."

"Amen," I repeated.

Tiara quickly squeezed my hand. "God wanted us to meet each other. Don't worry, He's going to show us the reason."

I didn't want to hurt her feelings, so I agreed. Just then, a nurse approached us.

"Jessica, a space opened up on the women's-only floor, so we're going to move you down. I'll go with you to your room and we can gather your things."

I thought this would upset Tiara, but she just looked at me serenely.

"We'll be together again soon. God has a plan for us," she said. And with that, she turned and headed back toward the dayroom.

CHAPTER 15

JESSICA BOTERO EKHOFF, ESQ.

———

I woke up in my new room on the fifteenth floor after a fitful night of sleep. I couldn't seem to keep my eyes closed, and I kept replaying the events of the first day in the ward in my mind, looking for clues. I needed to figure out how to get home to Dane and Wells. I had called Dane the day before and told him I was in some kind of experimental therapy program that was like a game with rules I didn't understand. He didn't confirm my belief. Maybe he had been instructed by the nurses not to tell me I was in an escape room. He was probably supposed to let me figure it out for myself.

A psychiatrist came to see me first thing in the morning. She checked my heart rate and blood pressure and asked me about my postpartum bleeding. Then she recommended I start taking a drug called Zyprexa to bring me back to my baseline. This alarmed me. I remembered what David had said about staff members of the ward pushing drugs. What if this drug was meant to make me docile and complacent so I wouldn't catch the wrongdoings of the nurses without any nail polish? I needed to keep my wits about me and stay alert. I might not be safe here, and I had to look out for myself.

Besides, what if there were side effects? What if I had a negative reaction? I thought about the time, a few years ago, when the dose of Zoloft I took for anxiety needed to be adjusted. The change was minor, but it sent me into a tailspin. For nearly two weeks I had some of the worst anxiety symptoms I'd ever experienced, even worse than after Whitney died. I trembled uncontrollably and my stomach roiled every time I tried to eat. I felt dizzy and off-balance, so much so that I was scared to drive. I barely slept. Instead, I lay on the couch in the basement, staring at mind-numbing home improvement shows in the hopes that the boredom would lull me to sleep. By morning, I was delirious with fatigue. I constantly felt like I needed to move my legs, and sitting still at my desk felt like torture. I'd close my office door, pull an old Snuggie out of my drawer, wrap it around myself as tightly as I could, and lay on the floor in the fetal position trying to take deep breaths. I'd listen to meditations on the Calm app, one after another, but they failed to bring any relief. I dragged myself through the work days, shaking and exhausted, counting down the hours and minutes until I could collapse into a ball in my living room. My body clearly responded poorly to changes in medication.

"It really is important that you start taking the Zyprexa," the psychiatrist said. "We want to get you home as soon as possible, but without the medicine you may need to stay here longer."

Was she threatening me? She knew how badly I wanted to go home. I had asked when I could leave as soon as she entered the room. My eyes immediately started watering when she told me it was too soon to know and we needed to take things one day at a time.

"How long would I have to take the Zyprexa?" I asked.

What if it was some kind of drug you had to take for the rest of your life once you started it? I didn't feel prepared to make that kind of commitment. I wanted to do research and get a second opinion. I wanted to talk to Jill.

Jill was my oldest friend and a nurse practitioner at an emergency room near where I grew up. Ours was a classic enemies-to-friends story. We met on the junior high track circuit. We both competed in high jump, and she always placed ahead of me. I was bitterly jealous of her. I loved high jump and put a huge amount of effort into it. I woke up early to practice before school, fine-tuning my approach path and jump mechanics before the sun even came up. But no matter how much I practiced, Jill bested me at every competition. We didn't talk at the meets, which I attributed to what I assumed was her arrogance, ignoring the fact that I didn't initiate conversations with her either.

My opinion of Jill as smug and self-centered had cemented by the time I signed up to go on a trip to Mexico with Jill's school's Spanish class the summer after freshman year. My own high school didn't offer any travel opportunities. Other than trips to Colombia to visit my family, I had never left the country and was eager for an adventure. My heart sank when I received the list of students who would be going on the trip and saw Jill's name. I hated the idea of spending ten days in close proximity to the girl who made me feel like a failure. But it wasn't enough to deter me from packing my bags.

On the third day of the trip, after studiously avoiding Jill, I was running late for the bus that would take us to that day's sight-seeing activity two hours away. When I scrambled aboard, I found the only available seat was next to Jill. I couldn't believe my bad luck. I braced myself for what I thought would be the most awkward bus ride of my life. But two hours later, I found myself entering what would become one of my most enduring friendships. Jill told me all about her four siblings and her boyfriend, who acted in local theater productions. I was taken aback by her openness and friendly demeanor. She was nothing like what I had thought at our track meets. We were inseparable for the rest of the trip. We marveled at the Aztec pyramids together, gossiped about the boy on the trip I had a crush on, and begged my mother, who was one of the chaperones, to take us to the famous Señor Frog's for virgin margaritas. Ten years after our friendship breakthrough, she was the maid of honor at my wedding.

    I wanted to ask Jill what she knew about Zyprexa and whether she thought I should take it. As soon as the psychiatrist left my room, I rushed to the phone mounted on the wall in the hallway. I picked it up but heard no dial tone. I looked at the clock on the wall. Phone hours weren't scheduled to begin for another two hours. The staff only turned the phones on during certain times of the day. But this was an emergency. The psychiatrist was asking me to take a medicine that might have grave repercussions. Surely I had a right to consult with the medical provider of my choice.

    I flagged down the first nurse who passed by in the hallway and asked her to turn the phone on for me. I explained the situation, and that I urgently needed to talk to Jill about the medicine recommendation I had received. The nurse, whose name tag identified her as Marcella, hurriedly told me what I had described wasn't an emergency and I could wait until regular phone hours to talk to Jill. Then she rushed off to a room a few doors down the hallway, where a patient was screaming incoherently.

I was stunned. My right to medical counsel had just been stripped away. This must be a violation of patient rights. I thought back to Marcella's hands, which had been holding a clipboard, and realized she wasn't wearing any nail polish. She was one of the bad ones. I had to do something.

I remembered seeing a poster by the nurse's station with the phone number of the hospital's patient advocate on it. The poster said patients could call the advocate to report abuse or mistreatment. I dialed the number the minute the phones were turned back on. I explained to the woman who answered the phone that I had been denied my right to consult with my chosen medical provider. I said that I thought Marcella wasn't qualified to be a nurse and should be removed from her position before she could cause any more damage. I told the woman that, as an attorney, I felt particularly well-suited to judge other people's ethics, or lack thereof, and I felt Marcella's refusal to let me talk to Jill was cruel and unethical. The woman assured me they would investigate the situation and gave me a claim number. I hung up the phone feeling vindicated. I felt certain Marcella would be fired and I had saved my fellow patients from her evil ways.

But there was a problem. The other patients may not have seen the sign with the patient advocate's number. They may be mistreated by Marcella or one of the other nurses without nail polish and not know how to report the abuse. As an attorney, it was my responsibility to keep them safe.

I rushed back to my room, tore a large piece off the brown paper bag that served as my trash can, and wrote with a crayon I had received from the supply closet: "I, _____, hire Jessica A. Ekhoff to be my attorney for one (1) week." I included space for my future clients to sign and date their contracts. This should allow me to represent them in any dealings they had with the patient advocate. I could also be present during any conversations they had with staff about their medicines, in case they suspected something improper was happening, like David said it often did. I admired my resourcefulness, then tore four more pieces off the brown paper bag and wrote up identical contracts.

I marched down the hallway with my contracts and crayons and sat down at an empty table in the dayroom.

"Sorry to interrupt, but I'm an attorney, and I'm holding office hours now. If anyone has any legal questions or concerns about your treatment here, you can come and talk to me," I announced. Murmurs spread throughout the dayroom.

A woman with close-cropped, blonde hair sat down across from me and eyed me suspiciously.

"You're really a lawyer?" she asked.

"I am," I said proudly. "Is there something I can help you with?"

"Maybe. I'm a photographer, and someone is stealing my pictures. I don't know how they're doing it, but they're getting into a folder on my computer, stealing them, and posting them on the Internet. It's been going on for months. I think they might be able to see inside my brain and know when I've added new pictures to the folder because as soon as I do, they end up getting posted. They're probably being sold for thousands of dollars, and I'm not seeing a cent of it."

I nodded sympathetically, but inside I felt pity for this poor woman. She was obviously having delusions. I should have realized not everyone in this place would be as clear-headed as I was. I didn't want to make her feel bad, so I decided to play along.

"That sounds really frustrating. But unfortunately, I think it's going to be a hard claim to prove. It sounds like you don't know who's stealing the pictures, so there's no particular person to sue. And if you sued for copyright infringement, you would have to prove the defendant had access to your pictures, so you'd need to know how they got them off your computer." I furrowed my brow and made my voice sound as sympathetic as possible. "I wish I had better news for you."

She sighed. "Well, it was worth asking about." She rose and returned to her chair on the other side of the room.

A young Black woman with her hair in braids immediately sat down. "Okay, so the first thing you need to know about me is that my birthstone is a garnet, so that's what I want people to call me. I'm Garnet," she said, pointing to herself.

"Okay, Garnet," I replied. "Then you can call me Sapphire. My birthday's in September."

Garnet smiled. "I knew I was gonna like you. So here's the deal. I love reading. Like, I'm obsessed with it. I can devour a book. When I came to this place, I didn't have any of my books with me, and it made me all depressed. Then I was walking down the hallway by the nurses' station today and I saw the bulletin board that talks about the 'soothing room.' Have you seen it?"

I nodded. The bulletin board advertised a quiet space that was open whenever therapy sessions weren't being offered.

"So the bulletin board has this big sign on it that says the soothing room has books. And I got all excited, thinking I was going to get something to read after all. But when I asked one of the nurses about it, she said they don't keep books in the soothing room anymore. But that just isn't right! You can't go around saying there are books in a place and then there aren't any books there. You see what I'm saying?"

I nodded. I felt anger on Garnet's behalf. The ward was stressful enough; the last thing anyone needed was to get their hopes up only for them to be crushed. The least the nurses could do was keep their bulletin board up to date.

Suddenly, a thought occurred to me. What if the nurses without any nail polish had done this on purpose? What if they were trying to get patients riled up so they'd throw a fit and then have to stay locked up even longer? I wouldn't put it past them.

"That's unacceptable," I told Garnet. "They shouldn't be lying about having books in the soothing room. I'm going to do something about this. I promise."

"That's what I'm talking about!" said Garnet, giving me a quick high five before any of the nurses could scold us for touching.

I realized after Garnet left that I had forgotten to have her sign a contract. But fighting to remove the false advertisement about books in the soothing room was a public service to everyone in the ward. I was essentially a class action lawyer acting on behalf of all my fellow patients. It seemed too burdensome to have everyone in the ward sign a contract with me, so I decided to make an exception and proceed without one.

As I was considering the next steps in the case, a woman in her early forties with dark hair in a ponytail sat down across from me.

"Hi, I'm Mary," she said. Her eyes were unnaturally bright. "It's great you're here because I have something I've been wanting to talk to a lawyer about." Her tone sounded rushed and urgent.

"You've come to the right place," I said. "How can I help?"

"So I was living in this place called Clayburn House for years. Have you heard of it?"

I shook my head.

"Lots of the girls here live there." She gestured around the dayroom. "It's horrible. They treat you like you're crazy, and they steal from you. They sneak stuff into your food too."

I furrowed my brow. "That sounds like a really terrible living arrangement."

"It is. That's what I want to talk to you about. I got kicked out of Clayburn a few months ago, and they wouldn't give me my stuff back. I have a bunch of clothes and toiletries there, and they say I can't prove they're mine. Plus, they've got at least two of my social security disability checks." The words tumbled out of her, each sentence faster than the one before. It was like she was up against a clock. Before I had time to respond, she went on.

"But the joke's on them because if they hadn't kicked me out, I never would have met DeMar."

"Who's DeMar?"

Mary beamed. "He's my fiancé. Officer DeMar Leland. I was living under an overpass on California Avenue right by the jail, and he used to walk by every day on his way to work. One day, he brought me a coat and told me he couldn't live without me. He said he wanted to divorce his wife and start a new life with me."

"We haven't been able to talk since I've been in this place, but I know he's waiting for me. I've got a ring picked out and everything. It's on layaway at a nice spot on Jewelers Row. And can I tell you something?" She lowered her voice and gave me a conspiratorial smile.

"He's not the only one I'm going to marry. It's going to be a three-way marriage with Barry Larson. He's this accountant I used to work for. He's the kindest man in the world. He's got a very soft heart. He used to call me 'Miss Lewis' like I was the most elegant woman in the world." She smiled at the memory.

"They're very different, DeMar and Barry. DeMar is passionate, and Barry is quiet. But I love them both in different ways. My ring is three gold bands intertwined to symbolize the three of us. I know it's not conventional, but I don't care what other people think. We're going to be very happy together."

She seemed to have completely forgotten about her grievance with Clayburn House. I found myself swept up by her romantic story. I wasn't sure if three-person marriages were legal in Illinois, but I decided not to mention that to Mary.

"When are you getting married?" I asked.

"We haven't set a date yet. We need to find a time when both of them can get off work for our honeymoon. We're going to Tahiti."

"I've heard Tahiti is beautiful," I enthused. "It sounds like a great place for a honeymoon."

I thought back to my honeymoon with Dane, almost nine years earlier. We'd rented a car in Los Angeles and driven up the Pacific Coast Highway, through Napa Valley and San Francisco, then up to Portland. Along the way, we stopped at beaches and vineyards and spent our nights in cozy B and Bs. An older couple paid for our dinner at an Italian restaurant one night when they overheard us telling our server we were on our honeymoon. It had been the perfect trip.

Mary's excited voice brought me back from my daydream. "Our honeymoon is going to be very important. It'll be the first time that DeMar and Barry get to spend time together. They haven't met yet."

I raised my eyebrows. "They agreed to get married without meeting?"

"I haven't talked to them about it yet," Mary admitted. "But I know they'll agree. They both said they love me more than anything and will do whatever it takes to make me happy."

I couldn't imagine marrying someone I'd never met, but Mary seemed confident. And she knew DeMar and Barry better than I did, so who was I to judge?

A nurse came into the dayroom to announce it was time for music therapy. Therapy on the fifteenth floor was much different than on the sixteenth. The patients didn't need to serve as therapists to each other. Instead, there was a full schedule of different types of therapy sessions each day, all listed on a whiteboard in the hallway. The classes included anger management, anxiety reduction, communication skills, and art therapy. I didn't feel like I needed any therapy, having already returned to my normal self, but my potential clients would all be in the class, and there was nothing else to do, so I gathered up my still-blank contracts and joined Mary in the therapy room.

The music therapist's name was Amanda. I noticed her pale blue nail polish right away and complimented her on it with a wink. I wanted her to know I knew about the secret code.

"Does anyone have a song they'd like to request we start with?" Amanda asked.

"'Hips Don't Lie'!" I yelled. "Let's hear from my fellow Colombiana!" I was energized by my idea of setting up a makeshift legal clinic in the ward and suddenly felt in the mood to dance. Amanda began playing the song and the sound of Shakira's voice filled the room.

"You're Colombian?" Mary asked. "You don't look like it."

I felt a stab of irritation. I hated having my identity questioned. It was like when I attended the first-day mixer for the SEO program in New York and one of the other participants—a girl with an obviously Hispanic last name—had asked me bluntly, "So what are you?" I didn't feel like I should have to prove I was Colombian.

"La gente siempre dice eso," I said in Spanish. "Pero soy Colombiana!"

"Huh! I never would have guessed it," Mary said.

I could feel the beginnings of anger stirring in my chest. I was just as much a Colombian as any other second-generation person living in the US. Arguably more, because I spoke fluent Spanish. But society didn't let me embrace that side of myself because my hair wasn't dark enough and my last name wasn't Latin enough.

Just as I was having that thought, another thought rushed in to replace it; I should change my last name. If I added my mother's maiden name, Botero, to my own, people would know I was Colombian without me having to prove it. Botero is the last name of one of Colombia's most famous artists, and the namesake of a major museum in the capital city of Bogotá.

I stood up from the table and started swaying my hips to Shakira's rhythmic voice. "I'm changing my name!" I announced to Mary. "I'm going to be Jessica Botero Ekhoff."

"That's pretty. When I get married, I'm going to be Mary Leland. It's important to DeMar that I take his last name. Barry won't mind."

I was too excited to listen to Mary. Why hadn't I thought of this before? It was such an easy way to solve the problem of not feeling like I was allowed to be Colombian.

I danced over to the table next to mine. "I'm Jessica soon-to-be Botero Ekhoff. What's your name?"

The elderly woman at the table stared at me mutely, but her disinterest did nothing to slow me down. I moved on to the next table and repeated my introduction.

"Jessica, why don't you listen to the rest of the song from your seat," said Amanda.

I shimmied my way back to my chair. "I'm Jessica Botero Ekhoff!" I cried, throwing my hands in the air. Then I smiled apologetically at Amanda and quickly sat down. I felt like a brand-new person.

CHAPTER 16

ARE YOU THERE, GOD?

After breakfast the next morning, I returned to my room to get ready for another day of seeing clients in the dayroom. I wanted to put my hair in a bun to look my most professional, but I didn't have a hair tie. Instead, I requested extra mesh underwear from the supply room and used the stretchy fabric to tie my hair up. I used a bit of the Curad ointment we had been given to moisturize our hands to shape my eyebrows and add a little shine to my lips. It wasn't perfect, but I admired my reflection in the mirror. I looked as polished as I could under the circumstances. Surely my clients would understand.

On my way to the dayroom, I stopped one of the nurses in the hallway. I checked to make sure she was wearing nail polish, then said, "I want you to know what a great job you guys are doing." I showed her my ID bracelet with my admission date printed on it. "I've only been here four days, and I'm already back to normal."

She smiled. "I'm glad to hear you're feeling better."

"I am. In fact, you'll probably see me out and about trying to help other patients. If you do and you think I need to go back to my room and rest for a while, you can just use the code word 'unicorn,' and I'll know what you mean." The psychiatrist had warned me that my blood pressure was elevated, and I needed to relax.

"It's very kind of you to want to help other patients, but you should be focusing on your own recovery right now," said the nurse.

"I did! But I'm already all better. Now I'm just working on figuring out the rest of the clues so I can go home."

The nurse furrowed her brow slightly. "If you're here, it means the doctors think you still have some recovering to do. In fact, why don't you head to your room now and get some rest? Maybe you could read your book."

"Books! That reminds me. I'm sure you're not the one who did it—I know you're one of the good ones—but you really need to fix that bulletin board about the soothing room. It says there are books in there, and people have gotten upset when they've found out there aren't any. It's not fair to get people's hopes up like that."

The nurse nodded sympathetically. "We used to keep books in there, but they kept getting destroyed. Patients would get upset, and they'd tear them up. It didn't make sense to keep replacing them."

"I get it. Not everyone in here is doing as well as I am. I understand I'm not your usual demographic. But I feel like it's my responsibility to stand up for the rights of the other patients. And right now, what I think you need to do is fix that bulletin board."

"It's busy in here today, but I'll see what I can do," the nurse assured me.

"Good," I said and headed back to my room. I trusted the nurse with the nail polish would do the right thing.

The day before, Dane had dropped off supplies for me, although I wasn't allowed to see him. He'd brought my softest leggings, a thick, geometric-pattern cardigan my friend Bren had lent me for breastfeeding, and a pair of wool clogs so I didn't have to walk around the hard tile floors of the ward in just my gripper-bottom socks. He also brought me a Fredrik Backman book, but my brain had been racing too much to read it. Instead, I was going to brainstorm ideas for solving the next clues, and maybe make a few more contracts for my new clients. The paper bag trash can in my room had been replaced after I ripped apart most of the first one for contracts the day before.

I picked up my notebook and a crayon. Pens, with their sharp tips, weren't allowed in the ward. I was about to start making a list of potential clues when I heard a loud buzzing sound. I looked up from my notebook, and the sound stopped. I turned back to the page, and the buzzing returned. That time, when I looked up, I spotted the clock in the hallway. It was exactly 10:00 a.m.—time for the phones to be turned back on. I had been so fixated on solving the mystery of the escape room and brainstorming ways to help my new legal clients that I kept forgetting about phone time. I had missed the last few opportunities to talk to Dane, and I knew he'd be worried about me.

Had the buzzing been some sort of reminder? Was it meant to keep me on track and ensure I stayed in regular contact with Dane? Suddenly, I froze. What if it was God? It had been many years since I had the sense that God was trying to communicate with me. What if He was using the escape room as a way to get back into my life? What if the whole reason I ended up in the ward was so I could rediscover God? Was returning to my Christian faith one of the steps to getting out of the escape room? Maybe Isaiah had been right and God really did want me back.

I dropped to my knees next to the bed and bowed my head. God, if that's really you, send me a sign, I thought. I heard the buzzing sound again, this time lasting longer than the first two times. I laughed giddily.

"It's you!" I cried. "God!" Tears began to prick my eyes. "I'm sorry I've been away so long. I've really missed you. I just didn't think I could believe in you anymore. So many people do such awful things in your name, and I don't trust the Bible because it was written by a bunch of men without any women's perspectives. But I realize now that I don't have to believe in the Bible to believe in you. The Bible is just a book, but you're God."

I thought back to the confirmation class I'd taken at the Lutheran church in eighth grade. It had felt like preparing for admission to an elite club. I remembered kneeling at the altar on my confirmation day and receiving a blessing from the pastor. I felt like I was receiving some sort of protective shield, a buffer against all the hard things in life. I was part of the church, and certainly nothing bad would happen to me with God on my side. Being a Christian was like having a top-notch insurance policy, and I couldn't believe how good it felt to get my membership card back after so many years.

The buzzing returned, and I wiped my eyes. "I hear you, God. I'm going to go call Dane. Thank you for helping me remember that getting home to him and Wells is the most important thing."

And with that, I put my mask back on and headed toward the phone.

*****

It had been a whole day, and no one had fixed the bulletin board. I had promised Garnet I was going to do something about the false advertisement for the books, and I intended to keep my word. I was a unique kind of patient—highly educated and privileged in so many ways, whereas many of the other patients bounced between family members' couches or stayed in homeless shelters. If I didn't stand up for these women, who would?

I selected the darkest crayon in my box and started down the hallway to the bulletin board. When I arrived, I raised my crayon to the large paper letters that announced "Books!" I paused and looked at the security guard stationed in his chair at the end of the hallway. He said nothing and didn't try to stop me. This must be another step in the escape room and he was assigned to watch me and make sure I completed it. Feeling empowered, I scribbled as hard as I could until "Books!" was barely visible. I felt proud of myself. I had done right by Garnet.

I was headed toward Garnet's room to give her the good news when I heard someone call my name. I turned around and saw Tiara, the woman from the sixteenth floor with an abusive husband.

"It's so good to see you!" Tiara gushed. "I didn't think I'd know anyone here."

"You made it to the promised land!" I joked. "Let's go sit in the dayroom."

We entered the dayroom and sat across from each other at a two-person table. A few other patients were in the room staring blankly at the TV, which was on mute.

"Guess what"? Tiara said. "They told me I'm getting out tomorrow."

"Really?" I felt a pang of jealousy. After much additional coaxing, the psychiatrist had finally convinced me to start taking Zyprexa. I thought I would be allowed to go home as soon as I started taking it, but two days later I was still in the ward with no promise about when I'd get to leave.

"Really. Now I just need to figure out where to go. I don't want to go back to Wisconsin. Jason would hunt me down." She shuddered.

"Is Jason your husband?"

"Yes, but he's going to be my ex-husband soon. I'm done letting him hurt me. He broke my arm once."

My eyebrows shot up. "Jesus Christ. That's awful. I'm so sorry."

Tiara nodded. "We were fighting, and he shoved me down a flight of stairs. I landed on my arm, and the bone broke in two places. I had to wear a cast for eight weeks."

"I'm so glad you're not going back to him. He sounds like a monster. Do you have any family you could stay with?"

Tiara shook her head sadly. "They all love Jason. They don't believe me when I tell them how badly he treats me. They say I'm exaggerating or just making up stories in my head."

"You deserve a better family than that."

Just then, an idea popped into my head. It was unconventional, but it could be exactly what Tiara needed.

"You should report Jason to the police and then join the Witness Protection Program."

"What?"

"Hear me out. They'd give you a new identity, and you could start over fresh. You'd never have to go back to

Wisconsin. And it sounds like your family doesn't support you, so who cares if you don't see them again? Good riddance."

Tiara's eyes widened. "Do you really think I should?"

I nodded emphatically. "That's what I'd do if I were you." Although I could never imagine a scenario in which Dane would break my arm, or my parents would side with him if he did.

"I don't know. It seems so drastic."

"This is a drastic situation." My voice grew more urgent. "You're a domestic abuse victim, and you have to do what you can to survive. No one is going to protect you unless you protect yourself."

My brain whirred with rage at Jason and Tiara's family and the abject unfairness of her situation. Another idea hit me.

"I could be your lawyer!" I declared.

"My lawyer?"

"Yes! I could represent you in your case against Jason and then help get you into the Witness Protection Program."

My work managing clients' trademark portfolios and clearing their advertising claims hadn't exactly prepared me for this type of legal work, but I could learn. I had all the resources I needed at my disposal. And God was on my side. I remembered what Tiara had said on the sixteenth floor about how God had put us in each other's lives for a reason. I realized she had been right.

"I think this is God's plan for you," I said.

Tiara stared at me. "Did He tell you that? Did God talk to you?" Her eyes were wide.

Just then, I heard a buzzing sound, and I immediately knew the answer.

"Yes. God wants me to be your lawyer, and He wants you to start a new life far away from Jason. You just have to trust me."

Tiara nodded eagerly. "I trust you. I know I can trust you if you hear the voice of God." She gave a surprisingly serene smile. "God will protect me. I know He will. He's sent you here to be His messenger."

"That's right." I could see how completely Tiara believed in God and His plan for her. Just yesterday I would have thought her simplistic and naive, but now I understood. Entrusting your future to God was an immense comfort.

"So, do you want me to be your lawyer?"

"Yes," she said quickly. "I'll do whatever you say."

"The first thing we need to do is get you a hotel room so you have somewhere safe to stay when you leave here tomorrow. You can stay there until I get released, and then we can come up with a plan."

I glanced at the clock on the wall and saw that the phones were turned on.

"Come on," I said to Tiara. "I'll call my colleague, Phil, and he can book the hotel room for you. I'll pay him back once I'm out."

Phil Barengolts had been my mentor at Pattishall McAuliffe ever since I was a summer associate. I had been so nervous about making a good first impression at the firm, but he had made me feel at ease immediately. He took me under his wing and staffed me on interesting projects, not the mind-numbing tasks often given to legal interns. He made me feel like my opinion was valuable, even as a junior attorney. Although we had technically become peers a few years ago when I was elected into the partnership, I still turned to

Phil any time I wanted a second opinion or to brainstorm a strategy. I knew he'd help me with Tiara.

I marched to the phone with Tiara at my side. I'd dialed Phil's number so many times over the years I had it memorized. The call went to voice mail.

"Phil, this is Jessica Ekhoff. I need your help with something. I'm actually in the hospital right now, which is why I'm calling from a weird number, but I'm fine. I'll tell you about it later. Anyway, I have a new client, Tiara, and she's going to be released from the hospital tomorrow. I need you to book a hotel room for her at The Robey for the next week because I'm not sure when I'm going to get out. I'll pay you back. Oh, and could you please also drop off a $100 Visa card so she can buy groceries? That would be great. Okay, thanks again, and I'll give you a call once I'm home to explain everything. But for now, I really need you to do this for me. Thanks."

I hung up and turned to Tiara. "Don't worry, Phil will take care of everything. You can trust him."

Tiara nodded. "I haven't stayed in a hotel room in years. I'm kind of excited."

"The Robey is great. It's in the middle of Wicker Park and there are plenty of stores and restaurants around. Plus, a Walgreens if you need any medicine."

"I'm going to go to my room and pack. I can't wait to get out of here tomorrow."

Tiara turned and headed toward her room. I smiled, feeling a deep sense of accomplishment. It felt good to be the unicorn of the ward.

CHAPTER 17

HOMECOMING

On my fifth day in the ward, I finally got the news I had been waiting for: I would be released the next morning. My blood pressure had gone down, and I wasn't experiencing any side effects from the Zyprexa. The psychiatrist was pleased with my progress.

That afternoon at lunch, I told Mary the good news. Mary had become my companion in the ward over the last few days. We had long conversations about DeMar and Barry and what I thought parenthood would be like once I got home. We walked the hallways like senior citizens doing laps at the mall. I had even invited her to host her bachelorette party at my uncle's picturesque farm outside of Bogotá, an offer Mary had readily accepted.

Mary squealed with excitement when I told her my news. "You're going home to your baby boy!"

"I know." I felt a well of emotion rise in my chest. "I've already missed a third of his life. Isn't that crazy?"

Because of COVID, visitors weren't allowed in the ward. But being separated from Wells when he was only ten days old felt so cruel. The idea of going back home to him made me nearly dizzy with excitement.

"I bet he missed his mama," said Mary. "Little boys need their mamas."

I thought of Wells, all wrapped up in his giraffe-print swaddle. I knew he wasn't old enough to smile, but I pictured him grinning when he saw me again anyway. I ached to nestle his little head in the crook of my elbow and stroke his cheeks. I wanted him to know that I'd never leave him again, that I hadn't wanted to leave in the first place. I didn't want him to feel abandoned.

Mary's voice cut through my daydream. "Can I ask you a favor?"

"Of course."

"I need you to go pick up my wedding jewelry. It's on layaway at James & Sons in the Loop. There are all our wedding bands, plus a watch for DeMar and a few gold bangle bracelets for me. It's about $2,000. I can pay you back as soon as I get out, but they keep telling me I'm not ready. I don't want the jewelry to get sold to someone else." She glanced around the room to make sure none of the nurses were watching, then grabbed my hand. "I know it's a big favor to ask, but it would mean the world to me." Her eyes looked urgent.

I nodded immediately. "It's no problem. I'm happy to do it."

I'd been thinking about money a lot lately, and the randomness of it. I'd always felt guilty for how much money I made doing something that didn't directly help people. Sure, companies needed to protect their brands and avoid getting sued for false advertising, but it wasn't like I was a cancer researcher or an advocate for the homeless. I enjoyed the mental challenges of my job and took pride in how hard I had worked to get it, but I also understood that what I did didn't have any real social impact. Yet somehow, for reasons that didn't make sense to me, someone had decided my job deserved to be highly compensated. As a result, I ended up wealthy—I liked to say upper middle class because it made me feel better but, in reality, I was wealthy—and uncomfortable about it. I wanted to be, as I had told the DoorDash representative, a good rich person.

    The night before I had been talking to my favorite nurse, Jasmine. I told her how impressed I was with the quality of the therapy program that had cured me so quickly. I told her I could see how hard all the nurses with nail polish were working, and that I thought they all deserved vacations. I wanted to pay for five days off for each of them. I asked her how many nurses worked each shift and how many shifts there were. When she wouldn't tell me how much a nurse earned in a week, I began doing my own calculations. I estimated that of the forty nurses who cycled through the ward each week, thirty were good ones, and I could give each of them a week off for about $25,000. I imagined taking the money out of our Ally bank account that was earmarked for emergencies. A vacation admittedly wasn't an emergency, but I felt obligated to use my money to do something good for the people who had cured me. It would ease my guilt about being an undeservedly rich person in the world.

    The same was true for Mary's wedding jewelry. I knew she had once been homeless and living under an overpass, so I assumed she didn't have much money. The $2,000 price tag attached to the jewelry was likely a huge burden to her. I decided I didn't even care whether she paid me back; this was just another opportunity to do something good with my money.

    It might also help me feel a bit better about not being able to help Tiara. To my surprise, Phil never called me back to confirm he had reserved the hotel room for her. Phil was steady and reliable, and I couldn't imagine what had led to this failure on his part. And I couldn't think of anyone else who would pay for the reservation. Something told me Dane wouldn't approve of me representing Tiara. He, like the well-meaning nurses, wouldn't get it, and would just tell me to go to my room and focus on my own recovery. None of them seemed to understand I was already recovered and now it was my time to use my privilege to help others. Mary's jewelry was an example of that.

Mary beamed at me. "Thanks, Little Sis. I knew I could count on you." Mary was about ten years older than me and had taken to calling me "Little Sis." As an only child, I was charmed by the nickname.

I took a crayon out of its box to write down the name of the jeweler in my notebook and saw a "Made in USA" designation on the back of the box. I heard a buzzing sound, and I gasped. I knew exactly what I needed to do.

A few years ago, I represented a client who had been sued for labeling one of its products "Made in USA." It turned out one component had been imported from China, which the class action attorney on the other side claimed was enough to disqualify the product from being identified as "Made in the USA." The law was vague, and there was room for argument on both sides. In the end, to avoid drawn-out litigation and the corresponding bad publicity, my client had agreed to settle the matter in exchange for an amount of money I thought was exorbitant. The members of the class each received small payments, but opposing counsel received a huge percentage. I had been stunned by how little work he had had to do to receive such a significant payday.

The buzzing sound I heard when I saw the "Made in USA" label made my next steps crystal clear; God wanted me to sue Crayola over their use of the "Made in USA" designation and use the settlement money they'd pay me to fund the nurses' vacation, Mary's wedding jewelry, and surely much more. Crayola was a large, well-established company with what I assumed were deep pockets. The amount of money they'd pay to make the lawsuit go away would likely be enough to fund several other socially beneficial projects. Maybe I could fund a special mental health ward in the hospital for postpartum women, where they wouldn't be separated from their babies and forced to ask male guards for mesh underwear as I had been. Maybe I could set up a legal fund so employees who were labeled as "independent contractors," like the Door-Dash representative, could sue for the pay and benefits they deserved. Maybe I could hire a prestigious law firm to help me in my battle against ABC. The possibilities were endless.

I told Mary my plan, and she said it was brilliant. I made a mental note to bring the crayons home with me the next day as evidence for my case.

I spent the rest of the day in art therapy, where we colored in adult coloring books, and an anxiety management class, where we did deep breathing exercises. Then it was time to pack. I carefully laid out my outfit for discharge day: a pair of soft black leggings and the cardigan my friend Bren had lent me. I had a feeling all my friends and family members would be waiting outside the hospital for me when I was released, and I wanted Bren to see I appreciated what she'd let me borrow.

I pictured discharge as a kind of graduation ceremony; I had made it through the escape room, solved all the secret clues, and won my freedom. Surely Dane would make sure all the people closest to me were there to congratulate me on my success. I smiled, picturing my loved ones with flowers and balloons. Dane would probably dress Wells up in a special outfit. I thought about what I should say to everyone who would come to celebrate with me. Maybe I should prepare a speech. I wanted everyone to know how grateful I was for their support.

I thought about what I'd say all through dinner and while walking laps with Mary afterward. I'd finished crafting an eloquent speech in my head by the time it was lights out in the ward. I knew the Zyprexa would knock me out like it always did, and I couldn't wait for the next day.

I woke up in time to see the sunrise. "That's a nice touch, God," I said aloud, looking up toward Heaven and smiling. I didn't hear the buzzing sound in return, but I knew God had heard me.

That morning at breakfast, I felt like a celebrity. Garnet announced to the room I'd be leaving that morning, and everyone cheered. Several women stopped by my table to tell me how happy they were for me. They all knew I had a baby waiting for me at home. I'd spent the last six days telling anyone who would listen about the unfairness of being locked up in the ward ten days after giving birth and not being allowed to go home, even though I'd fully recovered days ago.

A nurse came to my table and told me Dane was waiting in the lobby. I could leave as soon as I was ready. I gave Mary a quick hug after the nurse turned her back and waved to the other women in the dayroom. I was finally going home.

Another nurse handed me a bag with all the items that had been placed in the locker outside my room while I had been in the ward: the drawstring that had been removed from one of the sweatshirts Dane brought me so I couldn't use it to hang myself; my winter boots; my purse.

When I first arrived in the ward, I begged the nurses to bring me my purse so I could show them my attorney identification card inside and prove I was a lawyer. I thought they would surely release me if they knew what I did for a living. Lawyers didn't get locked up in psychiatric wards. We were privileged, special. The rules that applied to regular people didn't apply to us. But the nurses refused to give me my purse, and when I asked them to Google me so they'd find my law firm bio, they told me that would be a privacy violation. In the end, I had been treated just like everyone else.

In the elevator on the way down to the lobby, I practiced my surprised face. I was sure Dane had gone through a lot of effort to gather all my family members and friends to celebrate my graduation from the ward, and I wanted him to think I had no idea it was coming.

When the elevator doors opened, I immediately rushed to Dane, who was wearing Wells in a chest carrier. I saw Wells was wearing a regular blue striped onesie. But I reasoned Dane hadn't been given much notice of my discharge and likely hadn't had time to go to the store to buy Wells a celebratory outfit.

I looked over Dane's shoulder while I hugged him and was surprised to see the only other person with him was his father, who had been staying with him while I was in the hospital. I could see through the window that no one was waiting outside for us either. I almost asked Dane about it, but I didn't want to make him feel bad for failing to plan anything for me. This week had been hard on him too.

We left the hospital and started on the five-block walk home. I immediately noticed that everyone we passed seemed to be looking at us. Maybe they were hospital employees who had heard about my release and wanted to see me off, I thought. That had to be it.

I insisted we stop at my favorite café for coffee on the way home. Inside, there was a giant sign behind the counter reading, "We have avocados!" I gave God a silent thank you. Dane loved avocados, and the sign was clearly meant to welcome me back home to him.

We stepped back outside onto the sidewalk, and I turned my face up to the pale March sky. I had so much to do as soon as I got home. I needed to finish my letter to ABC, write a few posts on LinkedIn so my professional circle wouldn't forget about me, and do some research for my complaint against Crayola. All of that while being a good wife to Dane and a good mother to Wells. It was a lot, but I was up to the challenge. I could do anything. I was invincible.

EPILOGUE

As I write this epilogue, a twenty-month-old Wells gleefully dumps puzzle pieces in and out of their box and giggles as he pushes his scooter up and down the hallway. He demands a banana every time he sees one on the counter, and he never gets tired of going outside. His features have become more and more distinctive each month. He has grown from a generic-looking baby into a solidly built toddler with adorably tousled hair, long lashes, and my chin and smile. Watching his eyelids slowly flutter shut as he falls asleep in my arms at night is my favorite thing in the world.

The events that took place in this book feel almost foreign to me, like something that happened to someone else in a different time and place. In many ways I am back to the same person I always was, but in others I have changed permanently and for the better. Trauma leaves scars, but it also builds strength. A year and a half after the worst time in my life, I am more resilient, empathetic, and grateful than I have ever been. Which isn't to say my recovery was easy.

When I was first discharged from the psychiatric ward, I was still in a manic state that took weeks to fully fade away. My thoughts continued racing and tumbling around inside my head. I had too much energy and an inflated sense of self-importance, which combined to make me want to embark on countless ill-advised projects. For example, I reached out to a writer friend of mine who connected me with an editor at the *New York Times*. I pitched the idea of writing an article about my experience in the ward and was shocked when it was rejected. Rereading my email to the editor after the mania subsided made it immediately clear why I had been turned down. The sentences were long, rambling, and unfocused. The tone was hyper and somehow desperate. I sounded unhinged. I cringe now when I think about that email, just as I cringe when I think about my string of LinkedIn comments about the importance of supporting diverse attorneys and the incoherent GroupMe message I sent to my friends when I wanted them all to buy the COVID fundraiser hat.

It's also hard for me to think back on my relationships with David and, even more so, Mary. At first, I kept in touch with both of them. David and I planned to meet for coffee so he could explain the mechanics of what I still believed was the experimental, escape-room-based therapy program I thought we'd both completed. David kept rescheduling, citing last-minute work conflicts. Before we found a time to meet, my new medications had kicked in enough that I realized there was nothing special about the ward we had been in. I stopped calling David, and he stopped calling me. I think we each saw the other as a painful reminder of a traumatic time. It was best to close the door and move on.

I cut ties with Mary at the same time as David, although losing my connection to her was harder after all the heart-to-heart conversations we had shared. During my first week home, we spoke multiple times a day. She was still in the ward, and I dutifully called her whenever the phones were turned on. We talked about her wedding plans and her grievances against Clayburn House. She wanted to know all about Wells and Dane. She asked me to call the police precinct where DeMar worked and help organize a meeting between them when she was released. She said she didn't have a cell phone and couldn't communicate with DeMar once she got out of the ward.

I offered to get her a hotel room to stay in her first few nights out so she could use the room phone and make a plan for what she would do next. I went so far as to make the reservation, but then she told me she needed to stay in the ward for at least another week. By the time she proposed moving into my basement with DeMar and Barry after she was discharged, I had become lucid enough to realize she had a long recovery journey ahead of her and it was best for me to disengage. I felt deeply for Mary and her situation, but in the early days of my recovery I didn't have the emotional bandwidth to support her. I had to prioritize getting back to health. I knew from our many conversations that she had parents and a sister living in the city, and I trusted they would take care of her. As much as I wanted to help, I realized it wasn't always my place.

I began the Perinatal Intensive Outpatient Program at AMITA Health Alexian Brothers as soon as I got home. The program was as intensive as its name promised. Group therapy sessions were conducted four days a week, three hours a day. Because of the pandemic, the sessions took place over Zoom. There were around fifteen other women in the program at any given time, all of them pregnant or postpartum, and all of them struggling mightily. At first, I felt like the program was a bad fit for me because I was the only one who wasn't depressed. I completed my first day of therapy and complained to Dane that I had been surrounded by a group of downers. Marinating in the elated current of mania, I couldn't relate to the women on my screen who cried about feeling cripplingly overwhelmed and not connected to their babies. I felt powerful and accomplished. I put on a nice outfit and makeup every morning and silently judged the women in oversized sweatshirts and tear-reddened eyes. I gave unsolicited advice and saw myself as more of a therapist than a patient. I was flying high.

Then I received my diagnosis, and everything changed. The diagnosis was postpartum-onset bipolar I disorder with psychosis. What I had experienced was a severe manic episode. Apparently, the stew of hormones, new-parent stress, and lack of sleep had combined to activate a previously-dormant tendency toward bipolar that had been lurking within me. I couldn't wrap my head around the diagnosis. Bipolar people were crazy. They jumped off buildings thinking they could fly and went comatose when depressed. They killed themselves. Surely I couldn't be one of those people. I had a prestigious career, a successful marriage, and a happy childhood. No one in my family had bipolar disorder. In all the research I had done about postpartum mental health while pregnant, I never encountered anything about postpartum-onset bipolar disorder. It felt like an impossible diagnosis. It had to be a mistake.

But when the therapist walked me through the diagnosis criteria for bipolar, my heart sank. It was like the criteria had been written precisely to describe my first few weeks of motherhood. Delusions, like believing God was communicating with me through a series of buzzing sounds and that I was in a special escape-room-based therapy program. Inflated self-esteem and sense of importance, like thinking it was my responsibility to save *The Bachelor* contestants from abuse and help the other women in the psychiatric ward with their legal problems. Paranoia, like believing Dane was trying to have DCFS take Wells away from me. Decreased need for sleep. Racing thoughts and difficulty concentrating. Extreme irritability and rage. Every single bullet point described what had happened to me. There was no way to deny it; the diagnosis was right. Although I accepted the diagnosis was accurate, it devastated and angered me. Becoming a mother was supposed to be the most natural thing in the world, but somehow it had left me with a serious and lifelong mental health condition. I raged at the injustice of it and could barely stand to see pictures of other mothers smiling with their newborns. What gave them the right to have it so easy?

The diagnosis also terrified me. I didn't know whether it was possible to live a normal, fulfilling life with bipolar disorder. I joined a support group one day and felt my fear steadily increase as the participants shared their inability to keep their jobs, their multiple hospitalizations, and their rejections by family members and people they had thought were good friends. None of them seemed to be doing well. If this was the group of people I had been forced to join, then I was doomed. I panicked about what would happen to our financial situation if I could no longer work, and what it would do to Dane and Wells if I was in and out of the hospital for the rest of my life.

I was feeling a deep sense of despair about my future when another mom with postpartum-onset bipolar disorder, Kristen, joined the intensive outpatient therapy group. Kristen worked in IT, clearly adored her daughter, and made smart, insightful comments during group sessions. She didn't seem like a crazy person whose life was crumbling around her. We started privately chatting on Zoom, and I felt an immediate connection with her. Like me, she had no history of bipolar in her family. I was the first person with bipolar she ever met, just as she was for me. We both experienced mania within a few days of giving birth, and we were both hospitalized when our babies were just a few weeks old. I felt a rush of solidarity when I talked to her. Kristen understood exactly what I had gone through and could relate to me in a way no one else in my life could. She was positive and encouraging, and I cautiously started to believe that perhaps bipolar wasn't the death sentence I feared. If Kristen could have hope, then maybe I could too.

Another major source of hope came from the therapists in the intensive outpatient program. They were endlessly kind and always knew the right things to say. They assured me that millions of people live full, satisfying lives with bipolar, and I could be one of them. Over my nearly five months in the program, they helped me process the grief I felt about missing the first precious weeks of Wells's life and my sense of shame about having a highly stigmatized mental health condition. They taught me that one of the most important steps in recovering from trauma is finding a way to make meaning out of pain. I began to consider what I wanted to do to have an impact once I fully recovered.

A few months after discharging from the program and going back to work, I saw a Facebook post from a nonprofit called Postpartum Support International. PSI offered several resources I had taken advantage of while I was recovering. The most impactful was a peer mentorship program that paired me with a mom who had been living with bipolar disorder for years and who had become an invaluable source of advice and encouragement. She was confident, thoughtful, and generous, and became my first example of what thriving with bipolar could look like. Every time I talked to her, I felt a bit more hopeful about my future.

The post was seeking volunteers to lead fundraising walks in their communities as part of a global initiative called Climb Out of the Darkness. I immediately knew I wanted to get involved. This was my chance to do what the therapists had suggested and turn the worst time in my life into something meaningful. I found two co-leaders and set to work applying for a park district permit, finding sponsors, making an outreach plan, and handling logistics for the walk. The process invigorated me. More importantly, it gave me the courage to start being more open about my bipolar disorder. When people asked me how I got involved in the walk, I told them the truth. It felt good not to hide or put on a false face. I was honest about my experiences, and no one judged or rejected me, as I had feared.

The day of the walk was incredible. I was surrounded by friends and family, including several people who traveled to attend the event. Two of the therapists from the intensive outpatient program came. I got to hug them and look them in the eyes as I thanked them for getting me back to health when things seemed so dire. The most memorable part of the day for me was sharing my story. Standing in the center of nearly two hundred loved ones and strangers, I talked about the days of paranoia, delusions, and rage following Wells's birth, the hospitalization, and everything it took to get me back to my real self. When I finished, the audience burst into applause. I fought back tears.

By that point, I was almost finished with my first draft of this book. I started writing when I was six months postpartum. It began as journaling: a way to process everything that had happened to me during the first few weeks of motherhood and get all the thoughts floating around in my head on paper. But the more I wrote, the more I thought there might be value in sharing my story. When I first came home from the psychiatric ward, I was desperate to find firsthand accounts from other women who had experienced what I had. I wanted to feel like I wasn't alone and there was hope for recovery. I found essentially nothing. The lack of stories made me feel completely isolated and like I would never meet anyone who would fully understand what I had experienced.

I decided to share my story in the hopes of providing what I wish I could have found when I was at my lowest. I had two goals in writing this book: to educate people about postpartum-onset bipolar disorder, mania, and psychosis, which are rarely discussed, and to provide a sense of solidarity and hope for other women who have gone through what I did.

The process of writing this book was hugely therapeutic. Writing about what I experienced while manic helped me differentiate between my symptoms and who I am as a human being. I no longer feel guilty about the things I said and did while I was in a mental state beyond my control, and I trust my loved ones don't hold those things against me.

Writing the book also helped me deal with the shame and fear I felt when I received my bipolar diagnosis. We live in a society that stigmatizes mental health challenges, especially less common conditions like bipolar. When I first received my diagnosis, I didn't want to share it with anyone. I feared judgment. I worried about my colleagues thinking I was unreliable and other parents not wanting to leave their children with me for playdates.

When I started writing the book, I planned to publish it under a pen name to avoid outing myself as someone with bipolar. But over time, keeping my diagnosis a secret started to weigh on me. It added to my sense of shame to treat bipolar as something that must be carefully hidden. I didn't want to feel like I was putting on a false front, or constantly worry about accidentally letting it slip that I have bipolar.

So I chose to be open. I told all my friends and family about the book, which I published under my own, highly Googleable name. I've gone on podcasts and shared my story in detail in the hope of reaching those who need to hear it. I've posted about my experience on social media, including on LinkedIn, for all my fellow attorneys to see. The response has been unbelievable. I've been surrounded by encouragement, gratitude, and love. I've had strangers share their postpartum challenges with me and people I haven't spoken to in over a decade reach out to me. The support I've received from being open about my story has been the opposite of the isolation I felt when I was trying to hide it.

It would have been impossible to believe when I first received my diagnosis, but I love the person I have become through this experience. I am more empathetic and less judgmental, and my priorities have shifted in ways that have made my life richer. I am a multitude of things: survivor, advocate, mother, wife, daughter, friend, and a million others. The one thing I am not is a super sad unicorn.

ACKNOWLEDGMENTS

―

I've loved writing for as long as I can remember. I always dreamed of writing my own book one day but didn't know what to write about. I never could have imagined what the topic of my first book would ultimately be, but I'm incredibly grateful for the chance to share my story and shine light on a topic so worthy of attention.

One of the main reasons I was able to regain my health is that I am surrounded by so many incredible people, without whom I couldn't have recovered, let alone written this book.

First and foremost, thank you to my husband, Dane Canada. You are the best person I know, in every sense of the word. Getting to be your partner and raise Wells with you is the greatest joy in my life.

Thank you to my son, Wells Canada-Ekhoff, for turning me into a mom. You have helped reveal sides of me I never knew existed and taught me about a wholly new kind of love.

Thank you to my parents, John and Nohora Ekhoff (now known as Opa and Ita). You raised me to be strong, but also to know how to ask for help. You dropped everything to be there for me when I needed you most, and I've always known I could count on you. Thank you for loving me unconditionally.

Thank you to my father-in-law, Eric Canada. You were critical in helping us get through the early months of Wells's life, and you're an excellent Uda.

Thank you to my very best friend, Leigh Anne Haun. You are an endless source of encouragement, perspective, positivity, and laughter. I'm forever grateful to have you in my life.

Thank you to my fellow CHIEF Core members, Megan Nufer, Katie McKillen, Rachael Rohn, Jo Yocum, and Colleen Wilson. You cheered me on throughout this entire writing process, and you encouraged me to be brave and not make decisions from a place of fear. I published this book under my own name because you gave me the courage to do it.

Thank you to my colleague and mentor, Phil Barengolts. You saw me at my worst, but you stayed in my corner. Many people in your position would have treated me like a professional liability, but you never did. You're the best lawyer I know, but more importantly, an excellent person.

Thank you to the therapists, nurses, and staff at AMITA Health Alexian Brothers Perinatal Intensive Outpatient Therapy Program. You got me through the hardest time in my life, and you gave me hope for a better future when things felt so bleak. I hope you know that you change lives for the better every single day. You're miracle-workers.

Thank you to my therapist, Carla Marquina. Our conversations have helped me in countless ways. My life is richer because of you.

Thank you to everyone at Postpartum Support International, and especially to my Peer Mentor, Mikah Goldman Berg. You were my first and best example of someone thriving with bipolar disorder, and you helped me picture a full and meaningful future for myself.

Thank you to my publishing team at New Degree Press, especially Mozelle Jordan and Kenneth Cain. You helped turn an idea into a book I'm so incredibly proud of.

And, of course, a huge thank you to everyone who believed in me enough to order a copy of this book before it was even finished: Lance Pierce, Charlie and Jessica Davis, Zach Rivest and Kathleen Hannon, Sam and Mike Flora, Julia and Danny Imperial, John and Dena O'Hara, Mark Geiger and Sarah Page, Samantha DeFilippo, Katie and Lucas Blount, Amy Feltis, Daniel Muskovitz, Jessi Haramis, Sarah Leiser and Kyler Ransom, Dave Bremner and Carly Forsthoefel, Phil Barengolts and Anita Maddali, Angelina Spaniolo and Tyler Nall, Kyle and Katie Welter, Megan Nufer, Leigh Anne Haun, Alyssa and Jeff Pawola, Rachael Rohn, Katie McKillen, Lisette Zaid, Josh Parker, Cassidy Buzin, Marissa Kelley, Erin Espy, Dane Canada, Adrienne Hoffman, Jenna and Javier Cubria, Judy and Pete Olesen, Casey Potter, Happy Lakhan and Ankur Patel, Carla Marquina, Grego Urbina and Alicia Puig, Caity Scott, Meghan Hannon, Julia Horwitz, Kelly Graf and John Walker, Kim Walters, Rachel Dahl, Jeff Segneri, Eric Canada, Rachel Taylor, Laura Adair, Joelle Justus, Brian and Liz Hembd, Tiffany Gehrke, Annie Mygind, Jodi Neptun, Jennifer Kuzminski, Ashley Chung, Lily Becker and Max Hjelm, Jess and Brian Osmer, Bren and Alex Moss, Eric Koester, Erin Pudik, Nicole Niewald, Laura Perkins, Jake Fischbach, John and Susan Wasserman, Rachel Ternik and Matt Schiffman, Jill Cole, Jenna Goebig, Marie Roth and Tyler Olsen, Vanessa Luhr, John and Nohora Ekhoff, Jo Yocum, Meg and Chris Vandette, Denise and Ben Flowers, Jessica Karam, and Margaux Shain.

www.ingramcontent.com/pod-product-compliance
Lightning Source LLC
LaVergne TN
LVHW010325070526
838199LV00065B/5660